Stephen Fredericks

Loosing the Key of David

Key of David Healing Ministries LLC

Kennesaw, GA

Unless otherwise noted, all scripture quotations are from:

1) New King James Version of the Bible Copyright ©1979, 1980, 1982 by Thomas Nelson Inc., publishers.

2) The Amplified Bible Copyright © 1965, 1987 by the Zondervan Corporation The Amplified New testament copyright © 1958, 1987 by the Lockman Foundation. Used by permission

Loosing The Key of David
Copyright ©2008 by Stephen Fredericks
All Rights Reserved
Printed in the United States of America
Key of David Healing Ministries LLC., Kennesaw GA 30156

Dedicated to my loving wife
without whom I simply would not be complete.
(Nor in all liklihood would this book)

THANK YOU

Table of Contents

Introduction		1
1.	First Impressions	7
2.	Sins of the Fathers: Generational Sins	11
3.	In The Womb	17
4.	The Early Years (0-3)	23
5.	Performance Orientation / Procrastination	33
6.	Judging Parents & Others	43
7.	Inner Vows	49
8.	Forms of Replacement / Sibling Rivalry	55
9.	Bitter Roots: Judgments Create Expectations	63
10.	General Areas of Inner Healing & Deliverance	69
11.	Specific Areas of Inner Healing & Deliverance	81
12.	Deliverance, Casting Away Unclean Spirits	91
13.	Demerit Badges: Shame, Blame & Guilt	99
14.	How we See God / Forgiving Christians	105
15.	Soul ties, Formation & Severing	117
16.	Standing In Repentance	123
17.	The Homework / Follow-up	129
Bibliography		133

Welcome. Whether you have picked this up as a student of Inner Healing and Deliverance Ministry or you are just interested in the topic I pray this book is helpful to you. This is not a comprehensive guide to the subject nor is it meant to stand alone for instructional purposes. The basic structure of this book is organized in a chapter format which follows the basic structure of a ministry session(s); it is presented to give the reader insight into the processes of Inner Healing and Deliverance that my wife and I have had tremendous success with. Each chapter presents a topic; offers sample questions that tend to identify problems in the area, and sample prayers for leading a client to healing. Many of the questions may be repeated from one chapter to another simply because the same question may give insight into multiple areas needing healing.

"And the key of the house of David I will lay upon his shoulder; he shall open and no one shall shut, he shall shut and no one shall open." –Isa 22:22

For years I separated verse 22 from those that follow thinking that it was not part of the prophesy contained within them, but was rather an establishment of authority. An authority given because of what he would do for us in the following verses.

"And I will fasten him like a peg or nail in a firm place; and he will become a throne of honor and glory to his father's house. And they will hang on him the honor and the whole weight of [responsibility for] his father's house: the offspring and issue [of the family, high and low], every small vessel, from the cups even to all the flasks and big bulging bottles. In that day, says the Lord of hosts, the nail or peg that was fastened into the sure place shall give way and be moved and be hewn down and fall, and the burden that was upon it shall be cut off; for the Lord has spoken it." --Isa 22:23-25

This messianic prophecy in the book of Isaiah shows us a beautiful picture of what Christ accomplished for us on the cross. In verses 23-25 we see Jesus fastened as a peg in a firm place upon which "the *whole* weight of responsibility for his father's house" rests. He took the whole weight of the sin of the world upon him when he was fastened to the cross. From the smallest to the "big bulging" ones; no matter the issue He took it upon himself. And on that day when He was hewn down the burden that was upon him *was cut off;* for the Lord has spoken it.

It was not until very recently that I was given the revelation that the 'Key of David' was in fact the cross. When it was placed on Jesus' shoulder He was taking the responsibility for the Father's house. It is because of the work of the cross that He has been given all authority and all power in Heaven and in the Earth.

"…All authority (all power of rule) in heaven and on earth has been given to Me."
–Matt 28:18

So then when we loose the Key of David with which "he shall open and no one shall shut, he shall shut and no one shall open" we are in fact loosing the authority, power, forgiveness, grace and mercy of the work done at the cross of our Lord and Savior Jesus. It is by His sacrifice that our sins are forgiven. It is by His stripes that we are healed. It is by His resurrection and our confession of Him as Lord that we enter eternal life.

Where does Inner Healing & Deliverance come in?

Simply put Inner Healing is the evangelism of unbelieving areas of our heart. When we accepted Christ as our savior we became new creatures according to Paul in Corinthians 5:17. *Therefore if any person is [ingrafted] in Christ (the Messiah) he is a new creation (a new creature altogether); the old [previous moral and spiritual condition] has passed away. Behold, the fresh and new has come!* (AMP) and yet Paul also told us we were to *"walk out [our] salvation with fear and trembling"* (–Phil 2:12) and that we are *"not justified by [not knowing of anything we are guilty of]; but He who judges... is the Lord."* (ICor4:4 NKJV) How then do we reconcile these statements? To help clients understand I ask them if they have ever tie-dyed a T-Shirt.

If you're not familiar with the process I'll explain it to you. You take a plain T-Shirt, then twist it, tie it all up in knots and put rubber bands around it. Next you dip it in some dye. Now if we call that T-shirt the heart of one who accepts Christ and we call the dye the blood of the savior then when it comes back out of the dye we would say, "Look it's covered in the blood!" And we would be right in saying this. However, when we begin to loose the rubber bands, untie the knots, and unravel the twists we find all those areas the dye (the blood) didn't get to. You see those twists and knots represent the unrepentant and unforgiving areas of our hearts. The rubber bands are the strongholds of demonic influence keeping us bound up trying to prevent the freeing power of the blood of Jesus from completing its work.

Deliverance is the casting away of those demonic influences. Many believe that a spirit filled Christian can't be afflicted with a demon, but the more we follow after Christ and his will for our lives the more opposition we encounter. From where then does this opposition come? I am not saying that the person is possessed, just afflicted or oppressed in some way by an unclean spirit. The degree or severity of influence of these spirits varies by individual but it is foolish to think that we can do the will of the Lord without opposition in some form.

So we see, Deliverance is the removing of the rubber bands, the strongholds of demonic activity in our lives; and Inner Healing is the unraveling of our hearts so the freeing power of Jesus' blood can be applied to all of the areas we haven't given God. Inner Healing and Deliverance is a process. Beginning with the first session the client embarks on a journey of freedom moving from glory to glory receiving more and more freedom as they go. All of us are walking our healing / our salvation out with fear and trembling. *For now we see in a* mirror, dimly, but then face to face. Now I know in part, but then I shall know just as I also am known.—1Cor 13:12 (NKJV)

What Inner Healing & Deliverance is NOT!

Inner Healing and Deliverance is not: psychiatry, psychology, or therapy. It is not intended to take the place of any of these. It is NOT a self improvement program twelve step or otherwise. Every client that is seeing a doctor or other professional is told to continue to do so until said professional gives them the all clear. This does not negate faith in the ministry received. We are placing ourselves in agreement with Jesus own ministry, where time and time again He told those who had been healed to go and show themselves to the priests and be declared whole. We have clients share with their care provider what has taken place and then work together with them in gaining a clean bill of health.

The Session

While this guide is formatted to follow the general course of the ministry session there are some notes that should be shared about the session itself. This ministry has no set format. This is a Holy Spirit led ministry and as such can take many forms. I have ministered using this discipline at the altar, in street ministry, Sunday schools, conferences, one on one, and corporately. There is no hard fast rule for how it is to be done. The basic structure of the session does have some standard elements which are:
- The Interview
- Sharing
- Prayer

No matter the depth of ministry these three remain.

The Interview

The basic interview includes asking many key questions that will help shed light on issues that need addressing. Time permitting, as much information should be gained as possible to allow for the most freedom. As you ask questions let the Holy Spirit guide you. As the questions are answered always listen for the leading and guiding of the Holy Spirit. The Lord will give you insights as well as directing future questions.

Sharing

After the interview share with the client what you have discerned through their answers and the promptings of the Holy Spirit one subject at a time. Allow them the freedom to disagree with part or all of your assessment. If there is any agreement, move on to prayer. If there is none it is possible that they are not yet ready to receive or it is possible that we may have missed it. Even if we feel we have heard the voice of the Lord we must concede that we are fallible or that the timing is not right. If there is no agreement, apologize to the client and let them go; letting them know you are there for them and you are still their friend.

Prayer

If there is agreement continue forward leading them in prayers of confession, repentance and forgiveness. Some of the prayers you will lead them in, others you will pray over them. See the appendix section for the Session Outline for more information.

Other recommendations

Confidentiality is of the utmost importance. Never share information you get from a client with anyone else. Nothing will destroy your ministry faster than a client hearing something they shared in confidence coming at them from somewhere else.

Do not minister with a client of the opposite sex without another person acting as covering. A man should never minister to a woman without another woman present nor a woman minister to a man without another man present. This is for your own protection as much as it is for the clients comfort. If even one client makes an accusation of impropriety and you have no covering you have no defense. It becomes your word against theirs. Don't chance it. It isn't worth it.

Do not give advice. If advice can backfire it will. A client who has committed adultery may ask if they need tell their spouse of the infidelity. Either answer you give can come back and bite you. If you tell them no and the spouse finds out anyway the client will say "but that counselor told me not to tell you." If you say yes that same client will blame you for the destruction of the marriage either scenario paints you as the enemy and opens you and your ministry up to the possibility of legal action. Rather than give advice help the client to understand the pro's and con's of possible courses of action, leaving the decision between them and the Lord.

Don't go too deeply in a public setting. Clients may share, or the Holy Spirit may reveal, some very personal things, but some of these may be too intimate for a public setting.

If you plan to minister in this discipline and are not already part of an organization (church, organized ministry, etc.) I encourage you to form a legal organization. Incorporating, or forming an LLC protects you and your property from law suits. Have a "liability waiver / confidentiality statement" included in your new client packet. This protects both parties in the event of wrongdoing by either. Most of you will never need worry about this in the course of your ministry but we are living in a society that looks for reasons to sue. Jesus said, *"Behold, I send you out as sheep in the midst of wolves. Therefore be wise as serpents and harmless as doves." –Matt 10:16* (NKJV).

Chapter 1: First Impressions; The Handout

When we minister to a client we give them a handout outlining the four spiritual laws on which this ministry is founded. This handout also includes an often contested introductory statement. We begin this chapter with our foundational observation:

Your relationship with Father God is founded on your relationship with your natural father.

It is amazing the impact our relationship with our fathers has on us. It is our fathers who teach us what God is like. While our mothers give birth, providing physical life, it is our fathers who call our spirits to embrace that life. As the leaders of the home it is their responsibility to teach us right from wrong, to discipline us appropriately and to model for us how a man, a husband and a father ought to conduct themselves.

And you, fathers, do not provoke your children to wrath, but bring them up in the training and admonition of the Lord.—Eph 6:4

Train up a child in the way he should go, And when he is old he will not depart from it.
–Prov 22:6

If our father was not there for us growing up we inevitably feel as though God isn't going to be there when we need him. Likewise, if our father was abusive we feel as though God is just waiting for us to mess up so he can put us in our place. More detailed information on this subject will be covered in Chapter 14, titled "How we see God".

Four Spiritual Laws; The foundational basis for this ministry

Just as God weaved natural laws into the universe like gravity and inertia to govern our natural existence he has ordained spiritual laws to govern our spiritual existence. These laws are immutable and impersonal just like their natural counterparts. If you are convinced you can fly, whether you believe in the law of gravity or not, if you jump off a roof you are not going to defy gravity you are going to demonstrate it. It is a physical law. The spiritual laws that form the basis for this ministry are just as reliable.

1. The first commandment with a promise

Honor your father and your mother, as the Lord your God commanded you, that your days may be prolonged and that it may go well with you in the land which the Lord your God gives you.—Deut 5:16 (AMP)

The first commandment with a promise is to honor our parents. If we do so life will go well with us. The converse is also true, if we dishonor our parents it will go poorly for us and our lives will be cut short. It is possible you feel as though your parents weren't worthy of honor. You may have had dishonorable people as parents. Even if this is true it does not negate the command of the Lord. We are to honor our parents because of the position they hold as our parents. Our honor is not to be based on whether they are worthy of honor as people or not. Honor must be given because of the position they hold regardless of how they acted personally. One of the ways we dishonor our parents is through judgment.

2. The Law of Judgment

"Judge not, that you be not judged. For with what judgment you judge, you will be judged; and with the measure you use, it will be measured back to you."--Matt 7:1-2 (NKJV).

Judgment is criticizing, condemning, censuring, denouncing, and pronouncing guilt upon another. Judgment is a dangerous thing, because we cannot help but judge others by our own standards, or even worse our misinterpretations of God's standards. Jesus said his judgments were righteous because he wasn't seeking his own will but the will of the Father. When we judge others by faulty standards we end up seeking our own will.

"I can of Myself do nothing. As I hear, I judge; and My judgment is righteous, because I do not seek My own will but the will of the Father who sent Me." –John 5:30 (NKJV)

Our judgments tend to based in our perceptions of right and wrong. These perceptions are often based on our personal experiences. These experiences can begin in childhood and are then reinforced throughout our lives. Think about the nature of a child. Children make snap judgments, often with little basis in fact. Children do not have the reasoning capability to consider future consequences. They judge in response to their own will, as opposed to the "will of the Father". Because of their faulty judgment/assessment this pattern continues into adulthood, showing itself as condemning, censuring, and denouncing those things that don't line up with their way of thinking.

When a child judges a parent, that judgment doesn't end with them. It becomes a blanket judgment affecting all boys, girls, men, women, society, authority and even God. Therefore, if a boy judges his father he will become him in the areas he judges. If this same boy judges his mother he will reap these judgments through his future spouse. This is the nature of judgment and demonstrates the law of sowing and reaping.

3. Laws of Sowing and Reaping & Increase

Do not be deceived, God is not mocked; for whatever a man sows, that he will also reap. –Gal 6:7 (NKJV)

When we sow blessing we reap blessing. If we sow judgment we will reap judgment. No one sows tomatoes and reaps carrots. Furthermore, no one sows one tomato seed and reaps one tomato. Not only do we reap what we sow, our harvest is bountiful. The Prophet Hosea supports this when he says, "we sow the wind and reap the whirlwind." This is called the law of increase. When we sow a kernel of corn we don't receive a harvest of a single kernel of corn. We reap a stalk, with several ears, with hundreds of kernels of corn. As it is in the natural realm so it is in the spiritual realm. The judgments we make as children will bring a harvest of increase and the proportions will expand and grow throughout our lives. Our only hope is in the redeeming power of Christ. We need to ask Him to reap the harvest we have sown, not only do we ask that but we also look to Him to give us a glorious opposite. We Ask the Lord to up root the trees which bear bad fruit in our lives and to plant new ones, by His streams of living water.

He cried aloud [with might] and said, cut down the tree and cut off its branches; shake off its leaves and scatter its fruit. Let the living creatures flee from under it and the fowls from its branches. –Dan 4:14 (AMP)

he shall be like a tree firmly planted [and tended] by the streams of water, ready to bring forth its fruit in its season; its leaf also shall not fade or wither; and everything he does shall prosper [and come to maturity]. – Psa 1:3 (AMP)

4. Law of Forgiveness

Certainly one of the most difficult concepts on the earth is the concept of forgiveness. Peter struggled with this asking if he should forgive seven times. Jesus responded that he should forgive seventy times seven times. In fact in the Lords prayer he tells us to pray *"forgive us our trespasses (sins, debts, etc.) as we forgive those who trespass (sin, etc.) against us."* Whatever the translation, "forgive us as we forgive" remains the same.

Forgiveness is so important that at the end of this prayer forgiveness is the one thing Jesus goes back to explain as soon as He finished praying. *"For if you forgive men their trespasses, your heavenly Father will also forgive you. But if you do not forgive men their trespasses, neither will your Father forgive your trespasses."—Matt 6:14-15* (NKJV). If we want to be forgiven, forgiveness is not an option, it is a requirement.

This can be difficult because we may have a misguided view of what forgiveness is. Forgiveness is simply giving up your right to be angry with the one that has caused you hurt or offense. Forgiveness isn't saying that it's ok that someone hurt you. It is not saying that you are going to place yourself in a position to be hurt again. Forgiveness doesn't set the other person free it sets us free!

To better understand forgiveness it is helpful to understand unforgiveness. When we choose not to forgive it is like drinking poison waiting for the other person to die. Choosing not to forgive ultimately harms us. I have an example I like to use to illustrate this. Imagine you are driving down the freeway and someone cuts you off. You get really angry and even yell at them. Meanwhile they have continued driving down the road without giving you a second thought. You can't let it go so your anger festers and ruins your day, and they still haven't given you a second thought. Because he who angers you controls you, forgiveness becomes a lifeline since it will free us from the control of the other person.

Chapter 2: Sins of the Fathers; Generational Sins / Curses

"The Lord is long-suffering and slow to anger, and abundant in mercy and loving-kindness, forgiving iniquity and transgression; but He will by no means clear the guilty, visiting the iniquity of the fathers upon the children, upon the third and fourth generation."—Num 14:18

Beginning in Deuteronomy and throughout the books of the Law we find this recurring theme. God is willing to forgive but if we do not turn from our wickedness He allows the consequences to fall on us and up to three or four generations of our children. Just as obedience brings the blessing, sin will bring a curse. This is why when we sit with a client we ask what sort of illnesses, addictions, and mindsets can be traced back through the family line. Curses can be physical such as addictions or illnesses, or mindsets and behavior patterns such as stubbornness or abuse. This is why we call them Generational sins/curses, because they are passed down from one generation to the next. *emotional abuse*

This all started with Adam, the beginning of our generations, continued on through Noah and his children, and continues today. Physical and psychological curses can be passed down genetically or inherited as learned behaviors and mannerisms. Genetic examples such as Diabetes and Cancer can be traced medically. Mannerisms can include such things as parenting skills (or lack thereof), addictions, attitudes, and prejudices.

Is it possible to inherit sin? Some Christians say no. They argue that Jesus' death on the cross frees us from the problem of inherited trouble, but yet we clearly inherit blessings down from our forefathers, such as a strong gene pool, good health, longevity, good temperament, gifts, and talents. The benefits of civilization are inventions, sound investments, and wise decisions. The Lord does say that, *"each one will die for his own iniquity and without cause a curse cannot alight."* Ezekiel 18; Jeremiah 31:29-30; Proverbs 26:2. We also know that, in Gethsemane, Jesus took upon Himself the sins of humanity; nevertheless, our healing still requires confession, repentance and forgiveness of generational sins. Our experience in ministry confirms the need to address generational sins/curses, and we have ministered to many Christians who suffer generational effects. The fruit of a client walking in freedom is reason enough to accept generational sins as a reality for us today. The effects of Generational sins/curses may be due to ancestral bloodlines that have been polluted by unconfessed sin. Being freed from generational sin is a process and it can sometimes take more than one session.

There are three ways by which we can reap blessing or harm through what is sown by our forefathers:

1. **Through genetic inheritance.** Our DNA binds us physically and chemically to our forefathers. We inherit physical traits, illnesses passed through the genes, such as diabetes, hemophilia, even death itself was passed down from Adam as a consequence of his sin Romans 5:12.

2. **Through example or modeling.** It is well documented that environment influences behavior. Anger teaches anger, and resentment teaches resentment. What we see modeled in the family is written on our hearts. You will do to others what has been done to you; this is the reverse of Matt 7:12.

"So whatever you wish that men would do to you, do so to them, for this is the law and the prophets." Matthew 7:12

3. **Through the laws of God.** Judgment, sowing and reaping.

"Therefore you are without excuse, every man of you who passes judgment, for in that you judge another, you condemn yourself; for you who judge practice the same things." Romans 2:1 (NASB)

"Do not judge and criticize and condemn others, so that you may not be judged criticized and condemned yourselves. For just as you judge criticize and condemn others, you will be judged criticized and condemned, and in accordance with the measure you use to deal out to others, it will be dealt out to you." Matthew 7:1,2 (AMP)

Let me share my own personal story to illustrate the law of judgment, sowing and reaping. When I was growing up my father had abandoned me. My step-father was in the military, and he was a strict disciplinarian that believed the punishment should fit the crime. When I grew to adulthood and had sons of my own I found myself disciplining my own sons as I had been disciplined. I had vowed as a child that I would never deal with my kids the way my dad dealt with me (more on inner vows in Chap 10). Yet, I acted out the same behaviors my father had. What happened was as a child I had judged my step-father as abusive and harsh. In adulthood I reaped this judgment with my own children by subjecting them to the same treatment I received as a child. They would certainly have been doomed to reap the same with their children had I not severed the judgment and forgiven him, which effectively broke the generational curse.

Some examples of common patterns of generational sins are:

- Generations of alcoholism
- Tragic illness and premature death
- Multiple miscarriages/closed womb
- Financial and business failure
- Ancestors who have not stepped into their destiny or birthright due to fear, denial or rebellion
- Occult involvement
    1. Curses on family Deuteronomy 28:15 and following
    2. Unaccountable financial reverses
    3. Affliction through diseases, which refuse diagnosis and/or treatment and recurring ailments.
    4. Family feuds and unresolved conflicts
    5. There is a tendency to be drawn to the occult, even without knowing it; forms of prayer, visualization, and so-called Christian cults.

How to bring healing from generational sin

We break generational curses by repenting as Daniel did. Daniel stood in the gap for all of his people and ancestors, repenting for all of Israel when they were guilty of sin in Daniel chapter 9. When he humbled himself the angel Gabriel revealed himself declaring that his words were heard as soon as he began to pray and that the angel was sent to minister to him.

After leading the client to repent for all of their ancestors as far back as Adam who may have brought a curse on the bloodline it is then necessary to reverse every curse and call forth the clients blessing and birthright. We have the client bless the name of the Lord, bless Abraham, and bless his people Israel. In Genesis chapter 12 The Lord says to Abraham, *"I will bless those who bless you,"* (NKJV), so we bless Israel.

It is the birthright of every Christian to live a life of power and blessing. Equipped and established unto every good work. Therefore we lead the client to pray in every blessing, anointing, and calling that any of their ancestors left lying dormant, unwanted, or unused, calling these from the Heavenlies into their care.

Recommended Questions:

- What diseases / illnesses that seem to filter down either mothers or fathers side of the family?
- Was money an issue when your mother / father were growing up?
- Was anyone in your family involved in the occult?
- Was anyone in your family involved in the Masons?
- Does violence run in either side of the family?
- Does addiction run in either side of the family?
- Has anyone in the family history turned from God?
- What nationality are you?

Sample Prayers:

Have client Repeat: "Father, as Daniel repented for all of Israel, so I repent for all of my ancestors as far back as Adam who may have brought a curse on my bloodline. Father I repent for every ancestor who may have cursed your holy name. I repent for every ancestor who cursed Abraham. I repent for every ancestor who cursed your people Israel. Father I repent for every ancestor who cursed your plan for their life.

Heavenly Father I reverse every curse because I choose to bless your holy name, I bless father Abraham, I bless your people Israel. Father I embrace your plan for my life and that of my family in Jesus Holy Name."

Spoken over Client: "As you have repented for your ancestors as far back as Adam the Lord is severing every generational curse of (list specifics from interview). The Lord is severing from off mother's side and father's side as far back as Adam every generational curse. The Lord is loosing his angels to war in the Heavenlies on your behalf. He is loosing the key of David with which he shuts and no one opens and he is shutting every door the enemy has used to gain access to you through your ancestors sin."

Have client Repeat: "Heavenly Father I call forth every anointing, every calling, and every blessing, physical, emotional, spiritual, and even financial blessing that my ancestors refused to pick up, left lying in the dirt, Father I call them forth into my bosom. Father I call forth my birthright in Jesus holy name."

Spoken over Client: "The Lord is going back as far as Adam. He is gathering every calling, anointing, and blessing, physical, emotional, spiritual and even financial blessings, that your ancestors have left and he is placing them in you.

He is granting you your birthright in Jesus holy name."

Chapter 3: In the Beginning; In-Utero Encounters / Wounds

The Spirit of God has made me; the breath of the Almighty gave me life.
-- Job 33:4

But there is a spirit in man, and the breath of the Almighty gives him understanding.
--Job 32: 8 (NKJV)

At conception it is the Lord who breathes life into us. It is the Almighty who breathes our spirit into us with understanding. Not a cognitive understanding, as no brain has yet formed, but our spirit is present so this becomes a spiritual understanding. When God breathes our spirit into us He also instills an unspoken promise that we will be wanted, accepted, loved, cared for, and that we are the right gender. When the circumstances of our life here on the Earth contradict this promise we feel lied to, and stolen from. It is in this moment when spiritual rebellion takes place. Let me explain, everything a mother eats, drinks, or otherwise takes into the body while she is pregnant affects the child's body. Likewise every profound thought feeling or emotion she experiences will affect the spirit of the child. Just as smoking or drinking can have adverse physical effects, negative feelings such as fear, ambivalence, and anger can have detrimental effects on the spirit. The child's spirit, upon feeling these emotions, turns to Father God and says in effect, "God you made a mistake. I don't belong here. They don't even want me." God in turn responds, "I don't make mistakes. Your exactly where I've planned and called and have chosen you to be from the foundation of the world." This response is spiritual rebellion. Spiritual Rebellion in the spirit of an unborn child is a door that allows Satan access to mess with our lives.

Even from birth the wicked go astray; from the womb they are wayward and speak lies.
--Psalms 58:3

Well do I know how treacherous you are; you were called a rebel from birth.
-- Isa 48:8

Modern research confirms that there is active life in the womb.

Thomas Verney confirms Scripture in his book, The Secret Life of the Unborn Child; his extensive research indicates:

- Unborn babies hear, taste, feel and learn in the womb.
- Womb experiences shape a child's attitude and expectations about himself.
- Deep, persistent patterns of feeling in the mother affect the unborn child.
- Father's feelings about wife and unborn child also affect pregnancy.
- If the womb is friendly, a baby may be predisposed to good health, happiness and normal development; if the womb is unfriendly, the baby may be predisposed to ill health, nervousness, irritability, and arrested development.

Research indicates that babies are keenly aware of mother's feelings.

Ambivalent emotions such as wanting a child, but disliking pregnancy, or wanting to be a mother, but fearing the delivery, worrying about money, yet trusting in God to provide, creates confusion in the baby's ability to fully take hold of life. The baby may come forth listless, shy, or very reserved. They may be unsure of if, or where they fit in.

- There is evidence of remembered womb experiences, such as actual memories of birth trauma, induced labor, and breech birth.
- There are behaviors in infancy, childhood and adulthood, which correspond directly to known womb experiences.
- Verny reports on infants refusing to bond with mothers who rejected them in the womb.

Sound has an impact on the unborn.

- Quarreling, yelling, screaming, and loud noises can have adverse effects. It has been noted that music also affects the unborn child.
- Works by Vivaldi and Mozart are calming.
- Beethoven and rock music cause kicking, and violent motions in the womb.

Interesting study correlating abortion attempt and teenage suicide

One psychiatric study revealed a correlation between time of year when the mother tried to abort and the time of year the teenager tried to commit suicide. There was also a correlation between methods. It was noted that a mother's attempted abortion by sharp instrument, or chemical, correlated with the method of attempted suicide of the teenager; either by overdose or sharp object i.e., knifes razor etc. Research tells us that even the planning of an abortion does harm to the child.

Circumstances of Birth

One of the first insights gained concerning In-Utero encounters is revealed in the circumstances of birth. If the birth was traumatic, if illness or complications arose, if there were birth defects, even if the child was early or late can all be indications of wounding taking place in the womb. It is important to note that an absence of negative circumstances surrounding birth does not mean there are no wounds. The degree of wounding determines the degree of manifestation of symptoms. As an adult, it is possible to have made judgments and to have spiritual rebellion still operating without this initial sign of trouble. However, if there is trauma there is In-Utero wounding. The rule here is if there is fruit there is a root. The fruit may hide itself in a seemingly unrelated attitude or action, but as we follow the patterns and leadings of the Holy Spirit it will eventually show itself.

Effects of word curses

"Death and life are in the power of the tongue, and they who indulge in it shall eat the fruit of it [for death or life]." –Prov 18:21 (AMP)

"Out of the same mouth come forth blessing and cursing. These things, my brethren, ought not to be so." – Jam 3:10 (AMP)

Words have power. Every word we speak has the power to bless or curse the circumstances, situations, and people around us. Word curses are those negative statements that are given power when spoken aloud. Word curses spoken over us by doctors, nurses, technicians, parents, siblings, relatives and others can have terrible consequences. Word curses can range from gender confusion ("I hope it's a boy!" when in fact the child is a girl), to speaking death over the child ("I hope I'm not pregnant." "Now is not a good time to have a baby"). No matter how innocent the intentions of those speaking, these words are picked up by the spirit of the child and the damage is done. The encounters we have in the womb effect us well into adulthood. Lying, stealing, depression, suicide, inability to trust, homosexuality, and many other conditions can be directly traced back to the womb. For example, if a parent wants a boy but gets a girl, a child may purpose in their spirit to be what the parent wants and gender confusion or homosexuality can be the result. If the parent voices they hope they're not pregnant the child's spirit may be so wounded and rejected that a death wish is formed and the child can be miscarried, or become accident prone, even suicidal.

Word curses must be broken off and the lies replaced with God's truth. If we are acting out as a result of a word curse then our actions must also be repented of because it is based on a lie.

Recommended Questions:

- How many brothers and sisters were you raised with?
- What is the eldest's name and how many years older are they than you?
- Where were you in the birthing order?
- Any miscarriages before you were born?
- Do you know what kind of pregnancy your mother had with you? Were you early, late, or any complications?
- Do you ever feel as though you don't fit in anywhere?
- Do you feel as though there is greatness inside of you that can't get out?
- Do you find that you often sabotage yourself?
- Have you ever felt as though you didn't belong or fit in anywhere?
- Did you have a problem with stealing, or lying as a child, or even as an adult?

Sample Prayers:

Spoken over Client: "The Lord is going to your conception. He is the Alpha and Omega, the beginning and the end. Time and space can't hinder Him. He is omnipresent. He is at your conception and is holding in His left hand the egg and in His right ha[nd] cleansing the egg and the seed from all defilement, fear, ambivale[nce] (specifics from interview) (immorality if conceived out of wedlock). [Putting His] hands together, He is creating this wonderful union which is (client), breathing life into you and you into your mother's womb."

Have Client Repeat: "I repent for my spiritual rebellion and for opening any door that would give Satan an opportunity to gain entrance into me. I put my death wish and spiritual rebellion to death on the cross. I choose life and I choose blessings."

Ask permission to lay your hand on client's chest ... (If PDM is a male and client is female, have your female assistant lay her hand on female client's chest)

Spoken over Client: "The Lord is reaching into the depths of your soul and spinning your spirit within your chest, turning it forward until it is in direct alignment with your soul and body, so that you will receive directly from Father God all that He has purposed for you to receive, feel, and accomplish. I call your slumbering spirit to awaken in Jesus' name."

Mother's ambivalence:
- Everything your mother ate, and drank affected your body.
- Every profound thought and feeling affected your spirit.
- "I hope it's a girl! .... but money is tight."
- "I'm so excited! ... But will it hurt?"
- Ambivalence lays like a cloak across your spirit creating those ups & downs in your life It hinders you from continuing in a positive direction you get close to success & fall backward

Spoken over Client: "God is flooding your mother's womb with His blood ... cleansing it from all defilement and death. Heavenly Father, send your Holy Spirit to wash all ambivalence off (client's) spirit with the Blood of Jesus ... so their spirit can take hold of life as Jesus intended." If orphan spirit is present: "God is lifting up your orphan spirit that always feels like it doesn't fit in... where you always feel like you are on the outside looking in. He is nurturing you and holding you close ... saying this is your space, this is your place. "I ask the Lord to heal the trauma of your birth"

If conceived out of wedlock, have client cast "Bastard spirit" out. (If client is a child call it an "Illegitimate spirit")

Have Client Repeat: "As an act of my will and by the authority of Jesus Christ, I cast far from me the bastard spirit. I cast this spirit into outer darkness. Heavenly Father, send your Holy Spirit and fill the void that this evil spirit has left. Fill me to overflowing with your peace, joy, life, and light."

Spoken over Client: "Now I come into agreement with you...and cast this evil spirit into outer darkness, and invite the Holy Spirit to fill every void with His life and light in Jesus' Holy name.

Have Client Repeat: "I forgive all those who might have spoken word curses over me while I was in my mother's womb. I set them all free. I repent for buying the lie. I choose to receive the word of the Lord that I am fearfully and wonderfully made. I was called by my first name, before the foundation of the world, by my Father God according to His purpose and glory. I choose life, I choose life, I choose life, and I choose blessings in Jesus' holy name!"

Spoken over Client: "God is taking His sword and severing the umbilical chord between you and your mother He is clearing it of every hindrance and connecting it to Himself, so that His life can flow freely from Him through the umbilical chord into the depths of your soul filling you with hope, peace, confidence and courage."

Chapter 4: The Early Years; Our Earliest Reactions

"TO EVERYTHING there is a season, and a time for every matter or purpose under heaven" —ECC 3:1 (AMP)

"...Train a child in the way he should go, and when he is old he will not turn from it." Proverbs 22:6 (NKJV)

The majority of judgments we make are made in childhood. We do not realize this is what we are doing. Children see things very black and white and a natural response is often judgment. This is not necessarily a reflection of our parent's abilities / skills. It is directly a result of our responses to the direction and discipline we received. To help understand where, why and how some of these judgments are made it is necessary to look at the stages of human development.

Human growth requires certain accomplishments. These accomplishments occur in stages. Because these stages are consequential (important) as well as sequential (following in order), healthy and timely growth requires, as children, we learn them in the proper order.

The mental year

The term "mental year" is a means of measuring developmental accomplishments. This first mental year may be from 6 months to 3 years depending on the individual, but for this illustration 0-2 is considered average.

STAGES OF HUMAN DEVELOPMENT

In normal development, tasks are accomplished consequentially and subsequently. When one step is missed, it must be learned later. It is more difficult to learn something later on, because these stages are sequential and missing one step severely limits our ability to grow in the next. This is why we find so many adults still struggling in areas of individuation and initiative.

The following table gives the stages of development as well as the approximate ages when these skills should be learned.

STAGE	MENTAL YEAR	AGE
BASIC TRUST	1ST	NORMALLY 0-2
INDEPENDENCE	2ND	NORMALLY 2-4
INITIATIVE	3RD	NORMALLY 4-6
GANG-AGE	4TH	NORMALLY 6-12
TEENAGE	5TH	NORMALLY 12-19

Stage one: BASIC TRUST 0-2

This is the first and foremost of developmental accomplishments, without which the succeeding lessons cannot be well learned. Failure to acquire basic trust affects us throughout our adult lives, impacting our ability to relate to God and others.

Basic trust is the fundamental building block of all human relationships. If accomplished in the first mental year we gain:

- The ability to hold our heart open to others and life
- Security: the basic sense that "I'm OK, and loved."
- Resilience: the capacity to bounce back
- The courage to venture out, and take risks

- The ability to "shift gears", accept change, and bend without breaking
- Strength of spirit: having one's own center of decision; strength to discipline the mind
- To enter into relationships; to meet spirit to spirit; to enter into intimacy
- We learn basic trust from one primary experience

Trust is built as affectionate touch is received from both parents. It is especially critical to receive it from the father because he draws the child's spirit to life. Fathers teach children how to meet the world. Lack of affectionate touch can send a signal into the child's spirit telling them that their need will not be met, therefore they cannot trust.

"And you, fathers, do not provoke your children to wrath, but bring them up in the training and admonition of the Lord." —Eph6:4 (NKJV)

"He will turn the hearts of the fathers to the children, and the hearts of the children to their fathers," —Mal 4:6 (NKJV)

Disenfranchised fathers: A Brief History

Prior to World War 1, nuclear families were surrounded by extended families. When fathers went to war, uncles and grandfathers held the children; those generations developed basic trust.

Then came mobility: many families moved away from extended family to find new lives in other cities and states. The nuclear family became isolated.

Fathers went to battle again in WW II; this time there were no uncles and grandfathers close by to hold children. Even when they returned, many fathers came home wounded and/or had so much to do to catch up with schooling and careers, they didn't give the affection their children needed; thus, that generation did not receive basic trust.

When those children became fathers, they hadn't learned how to be true fathers and couldn't give affection, thus, succeeding generations could not give out what they never received.

Consequently, our society now suffers from serious moral breakdown. TV programs often portraying fathers as bumbling idiots relationally, while TV moms "have it all together."

Stage two INDEPENDENCE 2-4

Independence helps to achieve and accomplish basic trust, which includes the capacity to say "NO" even to those we depend upon for survival. It also gives a sense of Individuation (the ability to distinguish between "me" and "you")

The parent's role is to encourage rather than to crush a child's ability to say "no". Proverbs 22:6 tells us to *"train up a child in the way they should go."* This means noticing their natural bents and tendencies and supporting that. It does not mean willful disobedience is tolerated. A child needs to learn to obey, but we must take care to recognize their natural tendencies and adjust ourselves accordingly.

The limits of independence are defined by discipline. Children without proper discipline are left confused and lacking direction. Discipline and affection are both acts of love. Balanced discipline does not abuse. Striking a child when you are angry can lead to abuse, but striking a child is a necessary tool in the hands of a loving parent. When administering discipline, the level of punishment should match the crime.

Stage three INITIATIVE   4-6

Initiative is the ability to act upon one's own personal decisions. This gives us the capacity to enter and sustain peer relationships. If we have learned basic trust and independence, we can enter freely into the give and take of sharing emotions, thoughts, and space with others. Children first play along side one another; now they learn to play with one another. Children need to find security in themselves. If their security is determined by what others think, then they will be controlled by others.

Compliance and domination

Without initiative, children will either comply with or dominate others. The complying one (chameleon) goes along with everything. The dominating one fears the intimacy of give and take, and just takes. This leads to the tendency to treat people as objects.

Stage Four GANG -AGE   6-12

Children develop the ability to "belong" to a group of peers. This is normally characterized by a comparison or conflict between values and morals of an individual and of the gang. The emerging importance of "Peer Pressure" looms forth at this point. Experimentation and the acquisition of some adult life skills take place at this stage i.e., money management, the capacity to earn money by mowing lawns, babysitting, paper route etc.

It is good to encourage the child to start learning these skills now, so they can be developed by the time they are ready to step out on their own. In an effort to protect, or control our children we harm them by not teaching them to develop skills that will help them face the world and make mistakes on a smaller, safer scale. We want them to go out prepared to handle their own affairs. If the subconscious plan of a parent is to keep them dependent them for as long as possible, this will back fire. They may become dependant on someone out there that wants to control, or manipulate them. They may not take responsibility for their own stuff. Parents like this will do their children an injustice by not teaching them to be independent and teaching them initiative.

The "GANG-AGE STRUGGLE"

Without initiative (built upon basic trust and independence) the child tends to comply with peers, even when gang decisions are bad (fear-based). If a child has always complied with family values and morals, and does not have a healthy balance of independence and trust, it is likely that they will also comply with gang values and morals at this stage. Examples of area compliance might be clothing, sexual attitudes, language, and music.

You may walk into your child's bedroom one day and find that, that sweet loving, obedient clingy, hang on every word you say and think that you are the smartest daddy/mommy in the world has been replaced by the kid from hell. This new kid hates being in the same room with you. They got a communiqué that gave them the low down on all your shortcomings, hypocrisies, inconsistencies, and weaknesses. They have decided to point each one of them out at the most inopportune times.

Welcome to stage four. This is a normal growing and breaking away from parent dominants. If there isn't any of this going on then the parent might be too controlling and domineering. The child has not been allowed enough latitude to make mistakes share their feelings and has had to stuff emotions because it didn't suit mother or father. You might hear the parent say "You might be angry, but you better not let me see it!" The message is stuff and hide your emotions. This child has been so dominated and ill prepared for life that adulthood becomes a terror. The parent thinks that they have done a good job, because they look at other rebellious children who have put their parents through misery and they say, "Not my kid" as they have been made to toe the mark. What happens when they get out into the real world where life is trial and error? If they have been made to feel badly about themselves, if they have been made to feel that they are bad if they make a mistake, this child might settle for whatever they have, because fear of making any mistakes might paralyze them and keep them from growing into their full potential. Stuff your feelings, because you're not entitled to be angry, sad, fearful, etc. This adult will have a very difficult time re-learning what should have been taught by parents.

Stage Five TEEN-AGE   12-19

The teenager who has accomplished basic trust, independence, and initiative is on the brink of adulthood. They are able to enter into mature, equal relationships. They should be able to make important decisions based on a growing sense of right and wrong, and say "no" when appropriate. They should be able to accomplish two basic tasks:

Individuation: to break away from parental control and make their own decisions.

Internalization: to weigh everything that has come through parents, society, and culture then making their own determinations.

The struggle of teenage years

Gang-age problems multiply as modern teenagers face adult issues without appropriate skills. In contrast, adolescents of the Bible often worked at home, with father. He lived with the extended family, and was regarded as an adult on his 13th birthday, with Bar Mitzvah (Son of the Divine Law, commandment)

Teenagers should not be controlled like younger children. *"One who rules his own house well, having his children in submission with all reverence." — I Tim 3:4* (NKJV) refers to children under thirteen. If we try too hard, we as parents can turn individuation into rebellion especially if we are in the ministry. We as ministers must be careful not to parentally invert our children. When we expect them to act more adult-like, it steals their childhood, and makes them feel responsible for our success or failure as a minister. It sends a message that everyone will judge them by the way they act! Ministers let your children be children. The one thing that is consistent is that people will judge you any way.

Suggestions on how to deal with this age group:
- Begin to "let go". Fight the urge to be controllers.
- Offer trust and faith in your teenager, even when they have blown it.
- Offer affection freely.
- Talk about the mistakes that you have made

The loss of trust

Sometimes basic trust developed normally in childhood can be shattered later in life

- By sibling rivalries, and wounding
- Jealousies
- Economic troubles
- Being excluded "belonging issues"
- Teasing and ridicule
- Family position (I used to be the baby and now I got replaced)
- Abuse

Healing for lack of Basic Trust

- Offer affectionate and appropriate touch, which reaches beyond the present to the little one within.
- Have faith for the client, that God will provide what is necessary.
- Pray for trust to be rebuilt and restored.
- Support the client during the time needed to grow to maturity.

"...who through faith and patience inherit the promises." Hebrews 6:12

It is important to let the clients know that the Lord will never give up on them, no matter how many times they mess up. Failure is not messing up; the failure is when we quit getting up, or trying.

A common phenomenon accompanying the lack of basic trust in adults is late individuation. It will help to:

- Understand the problem
- Offer the necessary freedom for your mate to find their identity through (school, work, hobbies, etc.)

- Be a part of the learning process; share books, tapes, counseling experience, but don't try to teach them. It will come across as control and manipulation. If they do not expressly ask you for your help, then leave them to the Lord, and other trusted Christians.
- Pray that the Lord impart basic trust, independence, and individuation.

Before we can receive healing for these areas of our life it is necessary to own these areas of our life. We are required to own our lack of trust, our spiritual rebellion, those actions and reactions which are preventing us from entering into blessed relationships with our parents, siblings, society and even with God. When we take the responsibility for the decisions we've made without explanation or defense then we are able to release them to the cross and receive healing and freedom.

Recommended Questions:

- How many brothers and sisters were you raised with?
- Where were you in the birthing order?
- What is the eldest's name and how many years older are they than you?
- What kind of personalities did your brothers/sisters have i.e., angry, controlling, fearful, victims etc.?
- How do you get along with your children?
- Who did the discipline growing up? How would they handle it... with a switch, belt, or anything they could get their hands on?
- Would the other parent ever spank? How would they discipline?
- Did they ever lose control? Any unjust spankings?
- Were they ever abusive?
- Did you ever end up taking care of your baby sister/brother? Did you resent it? How old were you?
- Did you have any invisible friends as a child? Do you remember their names? (We are looking for familiar spirits)
- Any difficult or traumatic incidents in your childhood that trouble you now?
- Do you have any addictions?

Sample Prayers:

Spoken over Client: "When you were crying in the night needing to be fed, nurtured or changed... the caretaker might have been angry, frustrated, fatigued ... and the caretaker's touch sent a message into the depths of your soul that said, "My need is not being met or if it gets met, I will have to pay a terrible price." These messages formed a void in the bottom of the soul and you have been trying to fill this void throughout your life with people, places, and things (specifics from interview), and nothing has satisfied. And no matter how happy you have ever been, you can hear that echo saying it will never last for you. As I pray this prayer over you, the hand of God is going to seal this void, and He is going to pour in new wine, new oil, new milk, new bread, and the water of the Holy Spirit. And for the first time in your life, you're going to experience the comfort, peace, and joy of Almighty God.

(When you were crying in the night because of hunger, pain, discomfort. Your need got met, but the Caretaker's touch might have been, angry, frustrated, absent, or fatigued. The message to the spirit is, my need will get met, but I don't deserve it, not without me suffering some consequence, not without me feeling pain, guilt, shame. I must not deserve to have my needs met.")

Spoken over Client: "Lord, there is a little one deep inside (name of client) who is afraid, lonely, hurting, angry and hungry. They need to be held in arms, which are secure and strong. Thank you, Father, that your arms are like that, and that right now you are reaching deep down inside to enfold little baby name with the warmth and strength of your own being. I know that you, Father, are delighted with the little one whom you fashioned out of your own heart of love. This one, Lord, is chosen and precious, a treasure to you. You are pouring your sweet light into your child until all hunger is satisfied; all anxiety is settled out, all fears are calmed. Hold this one, Lord, until the love that you are permeates every cell of name being, and enables them to melt into you, trusting. Thank you Father, that you are light pushing back darkness; you are music displacing noise; you are a perfectly safe place to lie down and rest. You will never leave (name) nor will your love fail them."

(If the person is old enough to understand, have them repeat the following prayer after you)

Have Client Repeat: "Father, I take the responsibility for the choices that I have made, I confess attitudes which planted the original problems in my life, and I lay the entire matter on the altar of God, giving myself to You Lord without explanation or defense.

Father I thank you for bringing to death the old structure with its practices. Comfort and strengthen me from the inside, give me a new heart, and grow me up into the fullness of my new life in Jesus holy name. Amen"

Spoken over Client: "Lord Jesus, go back into (client's) life when the foundation of basic trust should have been formed, but wasn't. We ask you to comfort and nurture your child. Show them how much you cherish them. Build in them what has never been there... trust. Allow your blood to seal every breach, every break, and every chip. Let your love and solidity build that basic trust"

Have Client Repeat: "Father, I confess I do not trust. This lack of trust has hindered my walk with you and permeated my life. I know I must trust, but I cannot build it in myself. I forgive my parents for their lack of provision ... emotional, spiritual, physical, and financial. Now build in me that which was never there ... trust ... and restore the years that Satan has stolen, and I have squandered."

Chapter 5: Structures of Performance Orientation / Procrastination

"not by works of righteousness which we have done, but according to His mercy He saved us, through the washing of regeneration and renewing of the Holy Spirit" —Tit 3:5 (NKJV)

"who has saved us and called us with a holy calling, not according to our works, but according to His own purpose and grace which was given to us in Christ Jesus before time began," —2 Tim 1:9 (NKJV)

Performance Orientation was an issue I had to deal with myself. Growing up I judged that I could not please my father because he was very strict, and demanding. I felt nothing I did was good enough to meet with his approval. I had no idea what standards I was being compared to, and effort was not considered. No matter how hard I had tried or how much effort I had put into the task at hand if the results didn't meet with his standards then I would be required to repeat the task until it did meet with his approval.

I learned to be a "doer" to get approval, acceptance, love, and appreciation. I also learned that no matter how hard I tried to 'do' it wasn't going to be good enough. If by some miracle it was good enough it wouldn't last for me.

Performance Orientation has been an issue in the church from its birth. Paul, Timothy, Titus, James and John all address 'works' in their letters to the churches. Paul was probably the most outspoken.

"O foolish Galatians! Who has bewitched you that you should not obey the truth before whose eyes Jesus Christ was clearly portrayed among you as crucified? This only I want to learn from you: Did you receive the Spirit by the works of the law, or by the hearing of faith? Are you so foolish? Having begun in the Spirit, are you now being made perfect by the flesh?" —Gal 3:1-3 (NKJV)

The Galatians were trying to earn what could only be attained through Grace, and that is what we do. We try to *earn* affection, acceptance, love, grace, and approval, all with the knowledge in the back of our minds that it won't be good enough.

The constant tendency of the born-again believer is to fall back into striving to earn God's approval by human effort. Our minds and spirits know the free gift of salvation, but our hearts retain their habit to earn love by performing. We live unaware that motives other than God's love have begun to corrupt our serving through striving, tension and fear.

What is performance orientation?

Performance orientation is an acceptance of lies about us, built into our nature from infancy that propels us to strive to earn acceptance, approval and love through what we do or say. Our thoughts might go something like this:

- "If I do wrong, I will not be loved."
- "If I do not live up to family standards, I will not belong."
- "If I am wrong it means that I am bad."

Performance Orientation is doing the right things for the wrong reasons. Serving at church, helping friends and neighbors, and taking care of family in order to earn love, appreciation and acceptance from others and ultimately God.

Where does performance orientation come from?

- <u>Prenatal and birth trauma</u> can cause this situation. If a child feels unwanted, and tries to earn their place in life.
- <u>Lack of affection</u>, or lack of laughter in the home
- <u>Conditional love.</u> For example, during "potty" training (and other training) "You did good mommy loves you." "Yuck! Why didn't you tell mommy you had to do potty?" If I do good I am loved if I do bad I'm not!

- <u>Unwise discipline</u> which sends wrong messages. "Where did my nice boy/girl go? This can't be my little boy/girl…. "Go to your room until you can act like yourself; then you can join the rest of the family."
- <u>Family values.</u> Everything you do reflects upon this family. "There is a right way of doing things, and if a thing is worth doing it is worth doing right." "Our family does it this way." "
- <u>Competition and comparison</u> - Position in the family: first, middle, baby. "Why can't you be more like your brother/sister?" "Why aren't you as talented as your brother/sister?" Why aren't you smart like your brother/sister?

Recognizing the "fruits" of performance orientation

1. Rebellion – The person's anger is often suppressed and they may start to rebel.
2. Sabotage – Sabotaging successes in order to fail, reinforcing the lie they have embraced that they are destined to fail.
3. "Failure Attitude" – This attitude causes the child to work so hard to be what others expect that they lose their identity. They become angry that they must always perform to earn everybody's love (including God's). Affection, appreciation, admiration and acceptance are not freely given, so they know that they will never be good enough, smart enough, attractive, worthy, deserving, or lovable enough to earn it.
4. Workaholic Tendencies – Some have a need to "succeed." This person fears success as much as failure. They become a workaholic.
5. Perfectionism - Perfectionism stems from a fear of failure. The perfectionist has to get everything just right. If perfectionism goes unchecked it can become obsessive compulsive disorder (OCD). Both OCD and perfectionism are rooted in fear. The client must repent of fear and performance orientation to be set free.

Those struggling with Performance Orientation may:
- Strive for compliments, yet not accept them
- Not receive criticism
- Be compulsively defensive
- Take responsibility for everything
- Be overwhelmed, or over busy
- Tend to blame others
- Be tired
- Be angry (although sometimes hidden)

- Minister but cannot be ministered to
- Not receive gifts without reciprocating
- Try to control people and situations
- Be unable to be truly intimate
- Be lonely

Some results of performance-orientation are:

1. Fear
2. Striving
3. Insecurity
4. Compulsive need for approval
5. The center of every decision is based on what others think
6. Depression (see the depression cycle on the enrichment page)
7. Abusiveness (suppression/expression)

Performance Orientation in the Church

Performance orientation can affect more than an individual. We often see it manifested in churches where it becomes a "religious spirit." The religious spirit drives Christians to "works" in order to live up to the law, just as the performance-oriented individual performs out of fear and lack of faith in order to be accepted and to belong. It becomes a life filled with striving and guilt. When a church is infected with it, the body is condemned to live in fear of being cast out of the fellowship or even the sight of God unless they can do things "right."

"It was for freedom that Christ set us free; therefore keep standing firm and do not be subject again to a yoke of slavery."
—*Gal 5:1* (NASB)

Healing for performance-orientation

The individual must invite God to destroy this structure, and allow others to minister to them.

How to minister healing

Love the client unconditionally, as the Lord Jesus loved. Help the client to see that they have been doing the right things for the wrong reasons. Let them know that after they are set free they may be doing the same things, but their reasons for doing those things will change. Encourage them that they will be doing these good things because they love the Lord instead of doing them because they want the Lord to love them. Tell them they will be set free from the overwhelming need for the approval of people, because they will be no longer doing things for people's approval.

You will be able to see by the Holy Spirit the general patterns that flow through this individual's life. There is an "antenna" that is listening and focusing on the first sign of the offense, so that the client can say, "See! I told you that it never works out! I told you that I always get rejected, or turned against! All I ever do is try to help people and all that I ever get for my love, compassion and effort is dumped on.

I ask the following questions when I hear the client speaking in this manner. What is your reason for doing all of these wonderful things? Are you doing them as unto the Lord, or to get people to pat you on the back? Most of the time they will respond by telling you it is for the Lord. If that is so, (I ask) then why do you get so upset when the people you reach out to, turn against you? If you did it as unto the Lord, then you should feel good about yourself, because of your obedience, and the people's response should not have affected you. However, if you did it to be seen, or acknowledged by them, then I can understand why you would be upset. This then would be you performing knowing that no matter how hard you try it will never work out. This will get them to see that they truly have a P.O. structure.

Remember: Sins are washed away by the Blood of Jesus Christ, but habits, patterns and structures are Flesh and must be put to death on the cross.

When P.O. is strong a "Restriction" has formed around the client's mind, spirit, and soul that hinders them from walking into the fullness of God's love. Within every "Restriction" is a "Signaling Device" which sends out a signal 24 hours a day 7 days a week. The signal that is being sent out to everyone is (let the Holy Spirit lead you in this area) everyone picks on them; nothing ever works out for them; they always ends up holding the dirty end of the stick; every time they reach out to help somebody, or lend someone money they get cheated, taken advantage of or turned against.

Let the person know that they cannot fail as long as they don't quit. Let them know that it's OK to be wrong. It doesn't mean that they are bad; it simply means that they will have an opportunity to be right next time.

Help the client to hate the structures that were built into them. P.O. contains a reward system and therefore is difficult to give up. "If I do really well, everyone will like me." Pride can keep us from hating P.O. Remind the client that P.O. carries with it the baggage of "No matter how hard I work it will never be good enough."

Lead the person through confession, repentance, and forgiveness. Track the fruit to the root causes of the P.O. and lead the person into inner healing. Make sure they forgive those primary people who failed to give love.

After the client has forgiven everyone, we ask the Lord to sever the restriction that has hindered their walk of freedom, asking the Lord to crush the signaling device, and break the antenna that has been focusing on the bitterroot expectations (see chapter 9). We asked the Lord to sever, crush, and break restrictions, signaling devices, and antennas from birth to this age. Have them proclaim their freedom in Jesus' Holy name

Procrastination & Driven personalities

"Why do today what we can put off 'til tomorrow?"
– Procrastinator's Creed

"When you make a vow to God, your God, don't put off keeping it; God, your God, expects you to keep it and if you don't you're guilty... If you say you're going to do something, do it. Keep the vow you willingly vowed to God, your God. You promised it, so do it."
–Deu 23:21 (The Message)

Procrastination results from not being made a priority in childhood. The judgment is that mother or father were to busy to spend time with the child. The judgment doesn't end there however; it becomes a blanket observation of all boys, girls, men, and women, all society, authority and even God. The child grows up feeling they won't be a priority to anyone. Because the person suffering from procrastination was never a priority they are unable to establish, order, or meet priorities.

The structure of procrastination then works together with performance orientation to fulfill the prophecy that "we will never be good enough." Procrastination sabotages whatever success we might achieve. By putting off to the last minute those tasks we need to get accomplished we ensure that we won't have the time to do them properly and therefore we will fall under reproof, rejection, failure just like we expect.

When I was young I struggled constantly with deadlines. Homework assignments, term papers, chores, you name the task and I   put it off. Even into adulthood I struggled with this, though the nature of the tasks being shirked changed somewhat. I found myself chronically late for appointments or work, and I would put off chores until the last   minute. Though the manifestation of the problem had changed the   motivation remained the same.

Driven Personalities

Driven personalities consider everything a priority. Like procrastinators these individuals do not know how to establish, order, and meet priorities. Often those that are driven will push themselves to exhaustion performing for others. The thinking is that they will overcome any objections pertaining to the quality of work with sheer volume. If the quality is questioned the driven person responds with, "If you only realized how much I've got going on right now." or something similar. Driven individuals sabotage themselves by trying to do too much in the time allotted. They will schedule 12 hours of work for an 8 hour day, essentially planning their own failure.

Recommended Questions:

- Do you know what kind of pregnancy your mother had with you?
- What kind of personality did your dad have? How about your mom?
- Growing up, did you feel as though you couldn't please your mom/dad?
- How old were you when you accepted the Lord?
- If you died today, where would you be?
- If Jesus stood at the gate, and asked "Why should I let you into my Heaven?" What would your answer be?
- If you read the Word a little more, would God be more pleased with you?
- Is there anything that you know God has forgiven you for, but are finding it hard to forgive yourself?
- Have you ever had a hard time meeting deadlines?
- When Mom / Dad came home were they 'home' or did other things occupy their time?
- Have you ever struggled with tardiness? / Were you early for everything?
- Did you eat as a family growing up? At the table? What kind of conversation would take place?
- How would you spend time with your mom / dad growing up?

Sample Prayers:

Have Client Repeat: "We have judged our mother & father that we couldn't trust them. We judged that they betrayed us, stole from us, and lied to us.

(Explain being lied to and stolen from in the womb. An unspoken promise made at conception: that the child is loved, wanted, and made secure & safe. When it doesn't happen, the child is lied to and stolen from.)

Performance Orientation:

Have Client Repeat: "We took upon ourselves a structure called Performance Orientation where we have had to earn our right to live, earn our right to exist, earn everyone's love, acceptance, and appreciation ... including Yours Lord. But we knew we were never going to be good enough, smart enough, worthy enough, lovable enough, deserving enough. We pick up the Word of God like a sledgehammer and shatter the structure of Performance Orientation and we pick up the pieces and put them to death on the cross. We want to finally rest in the blessed assurance that Your love for us is truly unconditional ... not based on what we do, how good we are, how holy we are, but based simply on the fact that you can't help Yourself Lord. You have got to love us because you called us, chose us, and knew us before the foundation of the world. You knew what we were going to think, say, or do before we ever thought, said it, or did it and You love us anyway ... and we can rest in that."

Procrastination:

Have Client Repeat: "Father, we have judged our mother and father that we were never a priority in their life. Not in any boy or girl's life, man or woman, our children, our spouse (say their name), no authority's life, no society's life ... not even in your life Lord. And since we are not a priority, we cannot establish priorities, order priorities, or meet priorities. We use procrastination as a weapon to prove how unworthy we are. And if someone tries to make us a priority, we must prove to them, to God, and to ourselves how unworthy we really are. We must sabotage every relationship and self-destruct to prove how unworthy we truly are. We repent of this, Lord."

Driven:

Have Client Repeat: "Father, we have judged our mother and father that we were never a priority in their life. Not in any boy or girl's life, man or woman, our children, our spouse (say their name), no authority's life, no society's life ... not even in your life Lord. And since we are not a priority, we cannot establish priorities, order priorities, or meet priorities. We take on more than we can handle to prove how unworthy and incapable we are. And if someone tries to make us a priority, we must prove to them, to God, and to ourselves how unworthy we really are. We must sabotage every relationship and self-destruct to prove how unworthy we truly are. We repent of this, Lord."

Prayer for the structures above:

Spoken over Client: "As you have confessed and repented for these structures, shattering them and putting the pieces to death on his cross I speak the forgiveness of Almighty God over you.

Lord, just as Elijah called down the fire to consume the sacrifice, so I call down your holy fire to consume this structure. Father I pray that nothing remains of it for client to try to rebuild. Father I thank you that your love is sufficient and there is nothing we can do to earn it. Nor is there anything we can do to lose it but Father your love is truly unconditional and we can rest in that. In Jesus name Amen."

Chapter 6: Judging Your Parents

"Judge not, that you be not judged. For with what judgment you judge, you will be judged; and with the measure you use, it will be measured back to you."
--Matt 7:1-2 (NKJV)

"Therefore you are inexcusable, O man, whoever you are who judge, for in whatever you judge another you condemn yourself; for you who judge practice the same things."
--Rom 2:1 (NKJV)

Judgment can be a dangerous thing. In the church judgment often takes place under the guise of 'fruit inspection.' The word does say "we will know them by their fruits" in Matthew 7. But since we cannot know the hearts of men, passing judgment merely by observation can be wrong. We are told in I Corinthians 5 that we are to pass judgment (censuring disciplinary action) within the church according to the facts of a matter. But Christ warns us why we must be careful in our judgment.

"You [set yourselves up to] judge according to the flesh (by what you see). [You condemn by external, human standards.] I do not [set Myself up to] judge or condemn or sentence anyone. Yet even if I do judge, My judgment is true [My decision is right]; for I am not alone [in making it], but [there are two of Us] I and the Father, Who sent Me."
–John 8:15-16 (AMP)

Jesus warns us in this passage not to judge "by what [we] see, or to condemn by external human standards." This is because we only see in part, so judging the whole will be a judgment made in error. There is a story I like to tell to illustrate this point.

> *A wealthy man had three sons. When they reached the age where the father must give the blessing he challenged them. "There is a tree atop the mountain in the east that I visited in my youth. I want each of you to visit the tree and report back to me what you find. The son that gives me the most accurate description will receive the blessing." So the three go about their normal routines and one by one make plans to visit the tree. When a year had passed the father again called the sons before him. "What did you find?" he asked.*
>
> *"Father, Last spring when you gave us this task I went straight away to the tree you told us of. The tree was just beginning to bud and all around was the promise of new life. It was miraculous." The first began.*
>
> *"NO!" interrupted the second son, "The tree was in full bloom with leaves of the deepest green and fruit so ripe it was almost falling off the braches. I tasted it and it was good."*
>
> *"You're both crazy!" the third retorted. "That tree was vibrant with hues of gold and red and all around was a blanket of the same."*
>
> *The father shook his down cast head. "Not one of you has described the tree I remember. The tree I saw was gnarled and dead then just as it is today. You have all failed me."*

When we judge a snapshot of someone's life we will inevitably get it wrong. Just like that tree, we all have seasons in our lives. When we judge we are taking a snapshot of an isolated situation and declaring the whole is like that. For example, if someone lies to me it is acceptable and necessary for me to hold them accountable for their actions by confronting them with, "You lied to me." This brings attention to the sin and may lead to repentance. It is another matter all together for me to say, "You're a liar." Calling them a liar goes beyond holding them accountable, it colors their character, past, present and future. There is no room for change or repentance in that statement. It can place the offender on the defensive and possibly drive them away from repentance.

Matthew 7 doesn't tell us not to judge at all; rather it is a warning. If you judge you will be judged by the same standard. Paul was keenly aware of this in his letter to the Corinthians.

"But [as for me personally] it matters very little to me that I should be put on trial by you [on this point], and that you or any other human tribunal should investigate and question and cross-question me. I do not even put myself on trial and judge myself. I am not conscious of anything against myself, and I feel blameless; but I am not vindicated and acquitted before God on that account. It is the Lord [Himself] Who examines and judges me." –I Cor 4:3-4 (AMP)

When we judge others we convict ourselves according to the scripture in Romans 2:1 (See Chapter heading).

Kids and Judgment

Parents don't mean to mess up their kids. Most parents do the best that they can with the information they have. Unfortunately despite our best intentions kids do get messed up. Even if we do most things 'right' we cannot control our children's reactions to our methods or instruction.

I remember clearly as a child how my father would 'make the punishment fit the crime.' I was eight when one afternoon I knocked my little sister down. I have no idea what we were arguing about. Certainly nothing important (I was eight and she six how important could it be?). The next thing I knew I was tumbling down the hallway. When I looked up trying to understand what had just happened my father was standing over me. I will never forget his words, "You're bigger than she is. I'm bigger than you are. How did you like it?" If I answered at all it was a muttered "Not very much." In that moment I judged my father that he was cruel and abusive.

When I had my own children I found myself repeating the same disciplinary practices I had despised my father for. I often heard myself saying those things my father had said to me. I had become what I judged. I was powerless to stop. It wasn't until I sought healing that I realized how strongly the laws of judgment and sowing and reaping operate in our lives and received my freedom. When we as children judge our parents we are sowing the seeds that will bring us a harvest of judgment in adulthood. We become what we judge.

Blanket Judgments & Expectations

Children see the world in black and white, and in terms of always and never. Adults realize rationally that no one but God is consistent enough to 'always' or 'never' anything. This however is the language of children. A parent can consistently give the child what they want but it is the one time they don't get what they want that the child will focus on. "You NEVER let me…" Such is the response of the child. Children make snap judgments, and these judgments sown are no less powerful in our lives simply because we didn't think about them. As Paul said, *"I am not conscious of anything against myself, and I feel blameless; but I am not vindicated and acquitted before God on that account."*—I Cor 4:4 (AMP)

When a child judges mother or father, the judgments create expectations that all boys, all girls, all of society, all authority, and even God will be the same. Remember that our relationship with Father God is founded on our relationship with our natural father. This is because as children our fathers represent all authority. We transfer all of our judgments and expectations from our fathers then to God.

Every time we experience the fruit of what we have judged it reinforces the judgment and makes our expectation grow that, "this is the way it will always be for us." It is as if we erect a spiritual signaling device and antenna on our heads. The signaling device emits a signal 360° around us, 24 hours a day, 7 days a week, 365 days a year, saying, "Go ahead use me, abuse me, reject me, everyone always does." Meanwhile the antenna waits to receive the first syllable of the first word of the rejection. When it picks this up our spirit cries out in us, "See! It happened again! It always happens like this. I guess this is my lot in life."

Wounded Spirits Seek Out Wounded Spirits

When a little boy judges his father he becomes him in the areas he judges. When he judges his mother he marries her. When a little girl judges her mother she becomes her and when she judges her father she marries him. Wounded spirits seek out wounded spirits to fulfill the judgments made in childhood.

We may be attracted physically, intellectually, or emotionally to another but in the spirit we are attracted to those that will bring us the harvest we have sown. We might say, "Wow their gorgeous, and so nice..." but our spirits are saying something entirely different, "Now here's someone that will reject me, put me down, be emotionally detached. Bring them on so all these judgments I've sown can be fulfilled!"

Bill grew up in a home with a demanding and controlling mother. She would nag constantly about chores or homework and he felt like nothing he did was ever good enough. When Bill grew to adulthood and was dating he couldn't understand why every relationship he entered ended up the same way. The women were so nice and accepting and laid back when they were dating but when the relationship got serious all of the sudden these formerly complacent women became demanding, manipulating and utterly thankless. He had not ceased in his affections or in his demonstrations of them and felt blindsided by the metamorphosis in these women. The laws of judgment and sowing and reaping must be fulfilled in our lives (short of repentance and God's grace). When Bill's relationships became more serious the judgments he had made in childhood began to grow bringing him the harvest he had sown. When I ministered to Bill the pattern became obvious to him. He repented and we broke the cycle in prayer and forgiveness.

Healing for Judgments

Judgments must be confessed and repented of. Parents must be forgiven. Similarly we must repent and forgive all boys, girls, society, authority, and God for the same. Finally every signaling device and antenna must be crushed and a new one erected sending out and receiving acceptance, love and mercy.

Recommended Questions:

- What kind of personalities did your brothers/sisters have i.e., angry, controlling, fearful, victims etc.
- Are your brothers and sisters married? If so, married more than once? (If yes) What broke up the first marriage? Other marriages... How is their current marriage? Are they happy? (Ask these questions for each sibling)
- Have you been married more than once? If so, what broke it up?
- If you could change one thing about your spouse, what would it be? What's the one thing your spouse would change about you?
- How do you get along with your children?
- Do you know what kind of pregnancy your mother had with you? Were you early, late, or any complications?
- What kind of work did your dad do while you were growing up?
- What kind of personality did your dad have? How about your mom?
- Were they ever abusive?
- Would mom and dad fight a lot? What would they fight about? Tell me how old you were, and then tell me what happened, and how you reacted.
- Growing up, did you feel as though you couldn't please your mom/dad?
- Who did the discipline?
- How would they handle it... with a switch, belt, or anything they could get their hands on?
- Did they ever lose control? Any unjust spankings?
- Would the other parent ever spank? How would they discipline?
- Did you ever end up taking care of your baby sister/brother? Did you resent it? How old were you?
- Any difficult or traumatic incidents in your childhood that trouble you now?
- Have you had any affairs? With a married person?
- Do you struggle with procrastination (putting off to the last minute those things that need to be done)?
- Did you have a problem with stealing, or lying as a child, or even as an adult?

Sample Prayers:

(Because the specific judgments vary in every case there is no specific prayer to pray. All judgments must be confessed repented of and forgiven)

Have Client Repeat: "Heavenly Father I confess I judged my mother to be, specifics from interview. Father I repent for judging her and I ask you to forgive me. Please come and reap all that I have sown."

Spoken Over Client: "As you have confessed and repented for judging your mother I speak the forgiveness of Almighty God over you. Lord we ask you to reap all that has been sown and to lift client out of this field of weeds and thorns and to place them in a field they did not sow, to reap a harvest they did not plant. Lift them out of darkness and into your glorious light."

Have Client Repeat: "Heavenly Father I confess I judged my father to be, specifics from interview. Lord I repent for judging him and I ask you to forgive me. Please come and reap all that I have sown."

Spoken Over Client: "As you have confessed and repented for judging your father I speak the forgiveness of Almighty God over you. Lord we ask you to reap all that has been sown and to lift client out of this field of weeds and thorns and to place them in a field they did not sow, to reap a harvest they did not plant. Lift them out of darkness and into your glorious light."

Have Client Repeat: "Father God, we choose to forgive our mother and father, siblings, every boy & girl, (my own children), every man & woman, my spouse, all authority, all society ... We even forgive You, Lord for putting us in this family. We forgive ourselves. Come Lord Jesus and reap all that we have sown. Give us a glorious opposite."

Judging Parents is so integral in the Inner Healing process that no one chapter can hope to cover all of the ramifications. It is interwoven in every other area of this process and as such will be discussed as it relates throughout.

Chapter 7: Inner Vows

"If a man vows a vow to the Lord or swears an oath to bind himself by a pledge, he shall not break and profane his word; he shall do according to all that proceeds out of his mouth." –Num 30:2 (AMP)

Inner vows are determinations set by the mind and heart within one's spirit. They are typically formed during childhood. The following excerpt from Transformation of the Inner Man by John and Paula Sanford will help illustrate the cause and effects of inner vows:

> A woman came to [the Sanfords] who could not bear a male child. Several times she had become pregnant, and had miscarried boys about the third or fourth month. Gynecologists could find no physical cause. She wanted fervently to give her husband a son. We asked concerning her life with her father, and could find some hurts, but her reactions did not seem great enough to create such a destructive, obviously psychosomatic condition. Her brother, however, was not like the usual sibling who teases because he loves. This brother was vicious, continually embarrassing and physically hurting her. Her father failed to protect her. She remembered then, at about nine or ten, walking beside a river, picking up stones, hurling them into the water, crying out, "I'll never carry a boy child. I'll never carry a boy child." That was an inner vow, a directive sent through the heart and mind to the body. Though the conscious mind had long forgotten, the inner being had not. Though she now wanted to give birth, the earlier programming was still intact and functioning.

They are those vows made in response to wrong doing or judgment against our parents. Inner vows made by determinations or directives in the mind and heart in the early years can be more powerful than bitter root judgments. Inner vows can be obstructions in our nature that restrict our feelings and actions by limiting our freedom in God. They may even obstruct physical development.

Hearts of Stone

"Do not harden your hearts." Psalm 95:8

A heart of stone is a defense mechanism, a hiding place we believe will protect us from hurt, but which in fact makes us the loneliest people in the world. The Church is filled with hearts of stone, people who can love and serve others, but who can't allow others to minister to them. Healing is hard work; it requires time and understanding and support of family and friends. Inner vows are outgrowths of hearts of stone.

"I will give you a new heart and put a new spirit in you; I will remove from you your heart of stone and give you a heart of flesh."-- Ezekiel 36:26

In order for us to have true fellowship with others and with God, He must break our hearts of stone. In our fallen condition, we build walls around our heart to protect us from hurts and offense. These walls are reinforced with every reoccurring offense, rising higher and higher around us keeping out the pain and the hurt. The problem is that what we built to protect us from pain becomes a prison. The walls of which keep us from enjoying fellowship and receiving love, acceptance, and affection. These walls erected around a stony heart are formed out of our earliest experiences of frustration and dissatisfaction.

- A baby lies in their crib, crying for attention or food and the mother responds by changing their diaper. The baby can't speak and frustration grows.
- A baby wakes in the night and cries, waking parents. The parents respond to the child's need with anger, fatigue and / or frustration. The parents' touch sends a signal to the spirit and the soul, and the child begins to build a wall of protection around the heart.
- A baby wakes and cries, but there is no response. This is the beginning of the opinion that the baby is not a priority in their parents' life.

The absence or presence of love, laughter, and affection in the home will determine the hardness of the heart. Recognizing the problem of a stony heart can be obvious in some cases, characterized by heartless, uncaring behaviors and selfishness. This condition is often hidden in Christians. On the outside you will see a loving, caring, serving believer who can minister, but on the inside of his heart cannot receive ministry from others and even has trouble receiving from God.

The impact of the heart of stone on others

- In families, a person with a stony heart cannot receive love and intimacy.
- They tend to sabotage themselves and their partner by putting them down.
- In the body of Christ the person with a stony heart tends to drive wedges, create strife, and destroy corporate unity.

The damage a stony heart causes the carrier

- The person with a stony heart can develop physical problems: The build up of stress, and breakdown of the immune system.
- Loneliness, isolation, and feelings of not being understood by others.
- Leaders with stony hearts can't hear rebuke. They usually have gaping holes in their armor; they can't heed warnings, and are subject to temptations and delusion. They also suffer from burnout.
- A stony heart in leaders can destroy a church.

The Bible tells us there is safety in a multitude of counselors Proverbs 24:6 those with hearts of stone have trouble availing themselves of this protection.

Inner Vows

Inner vows are one aspect of a stony heart. Although they are made early in life and are often forgotten, they act as directives, which control our responses to situations and people around us.

Examples of inner vows:

- I will never grow up!
- I will never get angry like my dad!
- I'll get mom back for doing that!
- I will always respect women!
- I will never allow that in my house!
- When I become a parent I'll never…

When I was a child I remember telling myself I would NEVER treat my children the way my dad treated me. As I shared in chapter 6 I had judged my dad to be cruel and I made a vow that I would never be that way with my own children. Certainly this is an honorable and noble thing. The problem isn't in what is vowed, the problem lies in our inability to fulfill the vow. Vows made in judgment carry the seed of judgment in them. The judgment must be fulfilled. It doesn't matter whether we have vowed the opposite or not. Vows, no matter how they are made or what their intent, take control out of God's hands and places it in our own. Effectively we choose our will as the will to be done saying to the Lord, "It's ok God I've got this one, hand's off."

Inner Vows work at odds with the Laws of Judgment and Sowing & Reaping. All of which must be fulfilled. The person with the inner vow struggles to prevent the inevitable reaping of the judgment sowed through shear will power ultimately failing when their strength gives out.

Because the Lord holds us accountable for our vows we not only must reap the judgment but the consequences of the broken vow as well. Thus Inner Vows are doubly damaging. Fortunately the Lord stands ready to forgive us on all accounts if we will repent for making both judgment and vow.

Inner Vows in Childhood

Inner vows are very powerful when made in childhood during the formative years, because they are often forgotten and thus have more power due to their unconscious and hidden nature. Because of this they are often difficult to identify. The bitter fruit appears to remain even after the root has been severed:

- Defensive habitual flight mechanisms
- Automatic anger
- Bitter root expectations
- Actions and words that trigger automatic reactions
- Anxieties and fears

When we judge others and vow never to do what they did, the vow often works in reverse according to Romans 2:1

Inner vows are harmful, even when they appear to be good.

- I'll be gentle with women just like dad.
- I'll never drink or smoke.

They can coerce us to fleshly righteousness

Yes, furthermore, I count everything as loss compared to the possession of the priceless privilege (the overwhelming preciousness, the surpassing worth, and supreme advantage) of knowing Christ Jesus my Lord and of progressively becoming more deeply and intimately acquainted with Him [of perceiving and recognizing and understanding Him more fully and clearly]. For His sake I have lost everything and consider it all to be mere rubbish (refuse, dregs), in order that I may win (gain) Christ (the Anointed One), And that I may [actually] be found and known as in Him, not having any [self-achieved] righteousness that can be called my own, based on my obedience to the Law's demands (ritualistic uprightness and supposed right standing with God thus acquired), but possessing that [genuine righteousness] which comes through faith in Christ (the Anointed One), the [truly] right standing with God, which comes from God by [saving] faith. --Phil 3: 8-9

When I had made the vow never to treat my kids the way my dad treated me I was relying on my own righteousness and strength. Both of which would fail (and did) if pressed hard enough. When they did I was not only broken about how I had treated my kids but I was more broken that I had failed in keeping my vow. The enemy uses our vows to accuse us. In our brokenness he throws them in our face, "Didn't you say you would NEVER do that!"

Hidden Vows

It is not necessary to remember making inner vows. If the client can recognize the fruit then by faith they must forgive those who have hurt them as well as forgiving themselves. Confess and repent for their sinful reactions that led to the making of the vows, and then renouncing the vows by the authority of Jesus Christ

"I will give you the keys of the kingdom of heaven; and whatever you bind (declare to be improper and unlawful) on earth must be what is already bound in heaven; and whatever you loose (declare lawful) on earth must be what is already loosed in heaven."
–Matt 16:19 (AMP)

Healing Inner Vows

Ask the client to give the Lord permission to smash every inner vow that they have made. Ask the client to give the Lord permission to smash every wall, maze or mask that the client has been hiding behind, defending and protecting them self. Have the client declare that they want God to be their protection, defense and very present help in the time of trouble. Have the client ask the Lord to remove their heart of stone and replace it with a heart of flesh, giving them a new spirit and cleansing them from all their impurities and idols, and moving them to follow God's decrees and to be careful to keep His laws.

Have the client see their self in Ezekiel 36:25-27

"Then will I sprinkle clean water upon you, and you shall be clean from all your uncleanness; and from all your idols will I cleanse you. A new heart will I give you and a new spirit will I put within you, and I will take away the stony heart out of your flesh and give you a heart of flesh. And I will put my Spirit within you and cause you to walk in My statutes, and you shall heed My ordinances and do them." (AMP)

Recommended Questions:

(Because most inner vows remain hidden it is necessary to gauge them by the fruit in the client's life.)
- Do you find it easier to pray for someone than to have someone pray for you?
- Do you feel the need to pray for someone who has just prayed for you?
- Do you ever feel isolated, alone?
- Do you find that people have a hard time relating to / understanding you?
- Do you remember any times in childhood when you said, "I'll never / always … when I grow up?"
- Do you reject people before they reject you?

Sample Prayers:

(Lead client in confession and repentance for their inner vows and heart of stone / inability to receive. Have client repent for building the strongholds around their heart after explaining to them that what they had built to protect them has imprisoned them).

Spoken over Client: "Heavenly Father, lift your child out of this stronghold they've built. What they meant to protect them has become a prison keeping them from entering into relationships with family, friends, and even with you Lord. Father now send your Holy Spirit like a flood to erode the foundations of these walls. Let your love, grace, mercy, and healing topple the walls of this fortress so that not one stone stands on another. Now Father, be for them a strong tower; for you are a strong tower that the righteous run into and are safe. You have called client righteous. Father replace this heart of stone with the heart of your son our Lord Jesus. Let their heart beat in time with his own."

Chapter 8: Forms of Replacement & Sibling Rivalry

"Joseph's brothers envied him and were jealous of him" –Gen 37:11 (AMP)

"NOW MIRIAM and Aaron talked against Moses [their brother]"—Num 12:1 (AMP)

Sibling rivalry is as old as siblings. Cain was jealous of Abel; Joseph was plotted against by his brothers. Miriam and Aaron were jealous of Moses. Throughout scripture we find accounts of sibling rivalry and competition. Older siblings feeing replaced by younger. The younger feeling they must compete for the affection and affirmation they crave.

Many developmental psychologists agree that having at least a two year span between children is helpful to the development of both children. When siblings are not separated by at least this amount of time the older tends to feel replaced by the younger. The younger sibling in turn feels compelled to compete for attention, affection, and acceptance by the parents. This often plays out in sibling rivalry.

Replacement

The older sibling in this situation feels replaced by the younger. The child judges mother and father that they aren't good enough, worthy enough, adorable enough, and they don't feel loved. Furthermore they judge the younger sibling that they took their place in the family. They tend to judge themselves as well. Jealousy and anger generally accompany these judgments.

The 'replaced' child feels every show of affection or attention toward the other sibling should have been theirs. They feel stolen from and lied to, rejected and cast aside. The parents haven't stopped showing them affection or attention but the 'replaced' child's perception is ALL of mommy and daddy's time is spent on the usurper.

Competition

While the older sibling feels replaced by the younger, the younger sibling feels thrown into competition with the older. The younger sibling has arrived in the family to discover not only are they not alone, but that their competition has a head start in forging their place in the family. The 'competing' child then proceeds to perform to meet parent's expectations and to earn affection, attention, and approval.

In severe cases this performance may include sabotaging the older sibling's efforts to have the same. In this case the child is not only seeking equal attention from the parents they are trying to take the parents attention from the older child as well.

For the 'competing' child every show of affection or attention toward the older sibling causes them to strive that much more for their share of the attention. The 'competing' child often feels that they will never get what is theirs. They are very susceptible to the structures of Performance Orientation and Sabotage.

Replacement vs. Competition

My sons were separated in age by only fourteen months, and they were the textbook case of sibling rivalry. When my older son had out grown the bottle he would constantly steal his brother's. It wasn't even that he wanted it; he just didn't want his brother to have it. To him the bottle represented attention he no longer received.

As they grew older this competition took other forms. If one liked sports the other refused to have anything to do with them. When asked about it each of them would respond, "That's his thing not mine!" It was if they had come to some sort of non-compete agreement when it came to activities, styles of dress, music. It seemed to have no limit. Unfortunately this included a relationship with the Lord.

When one of them started going to church regularly with friends the other tried to apply this agreement to this area as well. That's when I had to put my foot down. We all sat down and I pointed out this pattern in their lives. I was shocked to discover that neither of them had been intentionally doing it. In fact, it wasn't until I pointed it out that either of them realized it had been going on at all. This pattern had been going on for years unbeknownst to either of them. After some explanation and direction, both repented and are free from this unconscious structure that was operating in their lives.

Replacement / Competition in Adulthood

Left unchecked these patterns established in childhood will follow us into adulthood. We can become overly competitive at work and within our relationships. When we marry, our spouse will become our competition instead of our partner. We can feel threatened when extra help is brought in on projects we are a part of. We tend to resent advice and correction because any help offered merely illuminates our own inadequacies.

Parental Inversion

Parental Inversion identifies those children who have taken on the role of a parent due to one or both parents being absent or ineffective as a result of death, divorce, sin or immaturity. The child tries to take responsibility, to fill the gap, or usurp the parental role.

The terms Parental Inversion and Substitute Mate describe the identity taken on by a child when a parent is unable or unwilling to fulfill their role. A child who has taken on the structure of Parental Inversion will carry the weight of care and responsibility which should rest on the father or mother, and this wounding will drive them through childhood into adulthood, where it will reap destruction in the individual and their relationships with others.

God established an order to parenting; when it isn't operating, the result may be parental inversion. The child enters into fear, saying, "Who will take care of things?" The child will enter into striving, which is an impossible job for a child. The child becomes proud of their adult role.

This can be built into the child by the parent with statements like; "I can always count on you to listen." "You're the man of the house now." "I don't know what I would do if you weren't here!" The child feels like things are up to them! They lose their childhood.

…For children are not responsible to save up (make provision) for their parents, but parents for their children.
II Corinthians 12:14

The Bible tells us that parents are to take full responsibility for their children.

These responsibilities include:

1. Providing appropriate boundaries and discipline *"He (the deacon) must manage his own family well and see that his children obey him with proper respect" I Timothy 3:4*

2. Supplying the needs of the family. *"If anyone does not provide for his relatives, and especially for his immediate family, he has denied the faith and is worse than an unbeliever." I Timothy 5:8*

3. Calling up the special gifts of the child, rather than trying to force a child into what the parent wants them to be. *"Train a child in the way he should go, and when he is old he will not turn from it." Proverbs 22:6*

4. Modeling Godly living. *"A father tells his sons about Thy faithfulness." Isaiah 38:19*

Adults who have taken on the structure of "Parental Inversion" see themselves as:
- Strong people who help weak people
- Caretakers, and protectors
- Problem-solvers
- Life-givers

These adults may manifest this structure in the following ways:
- Inability to rest, but extremely tired
- Need to make everything work
- "Things will get done better and quicker if I do it myself." They tend to steal the initiative and gifts of others. They tend to "Ace out" spouse. (Instead of allowing spouse to be in on the decision making process, the PI tends to decide what is best.)
- Difficulty trusting others: mistakes and imperfections trigger the need to step in.
- Difficulty trusting God: They see God as weak and needing help. They have an inability to say, "I can't do this."
- Sense of pride, "noble martyrs"
- Unreasonable fear: "If I stop doing, my family's lives, my life, the world, will fall apart, and it will be my fault."
- Trouble handling confusion or disorder
- Denial: They have difficulty acknowledging when they are trying too hard or that they are pushy. They have trouble allowing spouse to function.

- Inability to feel. When troubles require attention, they turn off emotion and get logical; full of advice, but little "heart."
- Inability to be corporate and intimate with spouse and children. Although roots are with parents, fruits surface in relation to primary people in their life.

Substitute Mate

This condition is created when a parent relies inappropriately on a child of the opposite sex for emotional comfort, or as a confidant. If the spouse is still in the home it undermines this relationship. The offending parent will give a child information that they should not have to know, i.e., "You know, your father is not capable of supporting this family."

In the worst case scenario the parent relies on the child for physical satisfaction.

- Child sleeping in the same bed.
- Excessive holding and touching.
- Incest.

Symptoms of substitute mate:

- All symptoms of "Parental Inversion"
- As an adult, seeking fulfillment out side the home. This creates vulnerability to adultery.
- Usurping the parental role, or dishonoring the other parent. This can cause sexual dysfunction, Oedipus complexes, and sexual difficulties in marriage due to inappropriate feelings of guilt and shame. There is also a tendency to have intense but hidden hate and anger toward the parent of the opposite sex.

Substitute Mate is often a consequence of single parenting. Single parents must be careful not to put this expectation on their children. The church needs to fill the gap for these families, and the parent should ask for the help, setting pride aside.

Healing for these structures

Recognition: Help the client seek out and discern the truth regarding behavior and motives. Encourage the client to ask their spouse, friends, etc., to confront them when they exhibit behaviors. Have the client make themselves accountable to them.

Prayer: Lead the person to ask the Lord to forgive them for taking God's job. For taking a role that they should never have had.

- Confess the judgments against the parents for stealing their childhood, and putting them in a position to take on a responsibility that they should not have, and for judging God for being too weak to handle those situations in their life.
- Repent for making these judgments against God and parents. Repent for taking the role that was not theirs.
- Receive forgiveness: This is a structure, habit and pattern that must be taken to the cross. Once placed on the cross receive the forgiveness the Lord promises.
- Support: Encourage new behaviors such as calling parents (if possible) to say, "I love you". Ask them to be aware of trying to control spouse, parents, and co-workers. If they become aware of this behavior, tell them to own it to disown it! "I see this habit, pattern, and structure and I am helpless to stop it Lord, so I put it to death on the cross and I ask you to give me a glorious opposite. In my weakness is Your strength." Tell them not to condemn themselves over it, simply own it to disown it, and allow God to change them.

Because many symptoms of parental inversion resemble those of performance orientation, it is important to make some distinctions. Performance oriented people believe they must earn their right to exist. Their concern is self-centered; their actions are designed to give them a sense of worth in the world.

Parentally Inverted individuals are moved by a different motive: those of making things better in the family, and even the world. In this sense they are truly self-less and centered on others, taking false responsibility for the well being of those around them.

This is why, without understanding their own motives, people who have a structure of Parental Inversion can hardly bear to hear that their actions might hurt instead of help, or smother instead of give life. We must not accuse them of selfishness, for that would be unjust; instead, we must gently minister truth to these wounded hearts who try so hard to fix the world around them.

Recommended Questions:

- How many brothers and sisters were you raised with?
- What is the eldest's name and how many years older are they than you?
- Where were you in the birthing order?
- Any miscarriages before you were born?
- What kind of personalities did your brothers/sisters have i.e., angry, controlling, fearful, victims etc.
- Are your brothers and sisters married? If so, married more than once? (If yes) What broke up the first marriage? Other marriages... How is their current marriage? Are they happy? (Ask these questions for each sibling)
- How did you get along with your brothers / sisters?
- What kind of pregnancy your mother had with you? Were you early, late, or any complications?
- Did you ever end up taking care of your baby sister/brother? Did you resent it? How old were you?
- Were both parents present when you were growing up?
- Did anyone ever touch you inappropriately, if so, how old were you, and by who?
- Did you tell? How long did that go on?

Sample Prayers

(Have client Confess judgments/resentment for replacing/being replaced by brother/sister.)

Have Client Repeat: "Lord I have taken upon myself the structure of Parental Inversion, I repent for taking your job, and I pick up the Word of God like a sledge hammer, and I shatter the structure of parental inversion and put the pieces to death on the cross. Now I give you back your job Lord in Jesus name. Amen."

Spoken over Client: "You have taken His word like a sledgehammer and shattered this structure, placing the pieces on His cross. Now Lord I ask you to consume this offering with your holy fire that client couldn't rebuild it even if they wanted to."

Have Client Repeat: "Lord I have taken upon myself the structure of Substitute Mate, I repent for taking (mother's / father's) place, emotionally, spiritually, physically, and I pick up the Word of

God like a sledge hammer, and I shatter the structure of substitute mate and put the pieces to death on the cross in Jesus name. Amen."

Spoken over Client: "You have taken His word like a sledgehammer and shattered this structure, placing the pieces on His cross. Now Lord I ask you to consume this offering with your holy fire that client couldn't rebuild it even if they wanted to."

Have Client Repeat: "Father God, we choose to forgive our mother and father, siblings, every boy & girl, (my own children), every man & woman, my spouse, all authority, all society ... We even forgive You, Lord for putting us in this family. We forgive ourselves. Come Lord Jesus and reap all that we have sown."

Chapter 9: Bitter Roots: Judgments Creating Expectations

"See to it that no root of bitterness springing up causes trouble, and by it many be defiled." -- Heb 12:15

"I am not conscious of anything against myself, and I feel blameless; but I am not vindicated and acquitted before God on that account. It is the Lord [Himself] Who examines and judges me." – 1Cor 4:4 (AMP)

What are bitter roots, or bitter root judgments?

- They are our sinful responses to those things that have happened to us, planted deeply within us due to our refusal or inability to forgive.
- They are our sinful reactions to circumstances that occur in our lives.
- They are condemning judgments of other people.
- They are the inability or refusal to forgive someone.
- They are the operations of the unchangeable Laws of God, which cause us to reap in kind what we have sown.

The law applies not only to our conscious actions, known and performed outwardly, but also to what is lodged in our heart, repressed, unknown and unexpressed. Because of the law of sowing and reaping, once formed, judgments must bring results. Bitter roots, not brought to the cross, will defile. Bitter roots are perhaps the most powerful negative force in our lives, bringing destruction not only to us but also to those around us.

In a tree or plant, a root is an underground, hidden structure, which is a conduit for nourishment. For us "roots" are habitual ways we drink nurture from God, others, nature and ourselves. Our roots also lie beneath the surface, usually hidden to the adult mind. If we have bitter roots, we drink harm to our selves.

Bitter roots are not the hurtful or terrible things that happened to us. Nor are they the sins of those who have wronged us.

Bitter Root Expectations

A "bitter root expectancy" is a recurring habit of a self-fulfilling prophecy, by which we "push" people to fulfill our picture of the way we think things will go. The thought process may sound something like:

- "Women will always be controlling."
- "Men can't be depended upon."
- "No one ever listens to me."

When I was a child I judged my mother to be emotionally unstable. Whenever I tried to speak to her about virtually anything she would cry. The expectation that formed in my spirit was that all women were emotionally unstable. Because of this judgment I was unknowingly sending out a signal expecting all women to cry whenever confronted. My spirit began listening for the first sob so the expectation I had erected could be reinforced. I was so afraid of making my partner cry I would hide anything that might upset her.

Bitter Root judgments and Bitter Root expectations usually originate with parents, but they can also begin with other caregivers in our youth such as grandparents or teachers. The judgment is a seed planted in childhood often long forgotten by the one making the judgment. Only after the child has grown does the bitter root expectation bear fruit. Sown in childhood it is then brought to fruition in our adult relationships with spouse, authority, society and even with Father God. Ultimately, we get what we expect. When I judged my mother, I planted a seed that bore fruit in my adult relationships with my spouse and other women friends. I expected all women to be emotional and because the signal I was sending out was expecting this behavior, I drew to me women who would fulfill my expectation.

If there is fruit there is a root.

"For there is no good (healthy) tree that bears decayed (worthless, stale) fruit, nor on the other hand does a decayed (worthless, sickly) tree bear good fruit." --Luke 6:43 (AMP)

No fruit hangs suspended in mid-air. If there is fruit (failing relationships, procrastination, inability to keep a job, etc.), there is a branch (a stronghold of demonic influence), a trunk (a bitter root expectation), and a root (a judgment, sin, vow, or other cause).

People come to me with all sorts of 'bad fruit' yet insist that their parents were wonderful. By their description, childhood resembled something out of the popular shows "Leave it to Beaver" or "Father Knows Best." It is then that I look them directly in the eye and tell them that they are painting me a picture of a good tree when all I see is rotten fruit in their life. If the fruit is bad, the tree cannot be good.

Healing for Bitter Roots

"He cried aloud [with might] and said, Cut down the tree and cut off its branches; shake off its leaves and scatter its fruit. Let the living creatures flee from under it and the fowls from its branches." –Dan 4:4 (AMP)

Praying for the fruit only relieves the recipient for a season. The branch, trunk, and root are still intact and given time the fruit will grow back. When we lay the axe to the trunk we are severing the structures in place causing us to reap what we have sown. When we shake off the leaves we are dealing with those sinful patterns that give shelter to the "living creatures and fowl." These creatures represent the unclean spirits that have come to torment us, hiding in those dark, unregenerate places within us. Finally, scattering the fruit is taking those habits, patterns, and structures and putting them to death on the cross of Christ. Only after the tree has been thoroughly and sufficiently hewn down can the Lord plant us a new tree. This new tree will bear fruit worthy of being called the planting of the Lord.

"...that they may be called oaks of righteousness [lofty, strong, and magnificent, distinguished for uprightness, justice, and right standing with God], the planting of the Lord, that He may be glorified." –Isa 61:3 (AMP)

"And he shall be like a tree firmly planted [and tended] by the streams of water, ready to bring forth its fruit in its season; its leaf also shall not fade or wither; and everything he does shall prosper [and come to maturity]." –Psa 1:3 (AMP)

Recommended Questions:

(Any of the questions from Chapter 6 can reveal Bitter Root Judgments & Expectations)

- Have you been married more than once? If so, what broke it up?
- If you could change one thing about your spouse, what would it be? What's the one thing your spouse would change about you?
- How do you get along with your children?
- What kind of personality did your dad have? How about your mom?

Sample Prayers:

Spoken over Client "Now the Lord Jesus Christ is taking His severe sword, going down into your soul of souls and severing every bitter root judgment, severing every bitter root expectation. He is going back as far as your infancy and healing every trauma that you have ever suffered, emotional, spiritual, physical, and even sexual. He is pulling out of the Heavenlies every word curse spoken over you by anyone, including those word curses you have spoken over yourself ... and throwing them at the foot of His cross. He is severing every restriction that has kept you from walking in His freedom or the fullness of His life. He is crushing every signaling device and antenna that has been raised listening for the offense.

God is erasing every lie whispered into your ear, spirit, mind, and soul and replacing them with truth." "You are fearfully and wonderfully made" "Greater is He that is in you than He that is in the world." "My God shall supply all of your needs according to His riches in Glory by Christ Jesus" (any other Scriptures that God lays on your heart)

Have Client Repeat "I put to death on the cross every habit, pattern, and structure that has hindered my walk with You Lord, i.e. anger, rage, inability to trust, fear, negative outlook, procrastination, fornication, pornography, etc. (specifics from interview). Now give me a glorious opposite in Jesus' name."

Spoken Over Client "The Lord is erecting a new signaling device and a new antenna. This new signaling device is sending out the signal that you are worth taking the time to get to know. You are loved, accepted and worthy of their time, attention, and affirmation / affection. This new antenna is listening for the first syllable of the first word of need. Now that you have been set free He is positioning you to help others. The focus is off of how you have been or will be treated and is now on how you can be used by him to heal and help his other children. Freely you have received now freely give in Jesus holy name. Amen."

Chapter 10: The Common Struggle; Prayers of Deliverance (Common)

"No temptation has overtaken you except such as is common to man; but God is faithful, who will not allow you to be tempted beyond what you are able, but with the temptation will also make the way of escape, that you may be able to bear it."—1Cor 10:13 (NKJV)

There is no temptation that is not common to man, or in other words we all have stuff. That is not to say that we all have the same stuff but each of us is going through something. The encouragement in the above verse isn't that God will make a way for you to avoid the temptation; rather it is a promise that he will see you through it. We all have moments in our lives where we find ourselves walking *"in the valley of the shadow of death"* the Word doesn't say, "Yea though I walk *around / over / beside* the valley" it says, *through* the valley. When we try to avoid the painful situations in our lives we are ignoring the problem rather than facing it. We must take ownership of our problems before we can disown them.

The following are some of the more common struggles we encounter when ministering to clients.

Slumbering Spirit

"…The hour has come for you to wake up from your slumber, because our salvation is nearer now than when we first believed"-- Rom 13:11

A slumbering spirit is a condition in which the personal spirit has not been fully awakened, which causes certain facets of the person's life to lie dormant. We may be a believer, and yet there can be areas of our life where unbelief or the lack of emotion can present itself. While standing in the middle of praise and worship we may watch others expressing emotion but we can't feel anything; or perhaps agitation rises up when those around seem to be at peace when we are not.

I remember when I first encountered the Charismatic movement. I stood in the middle of the sanctuary surrounded by believers. All of them had their hands raised to God, worshipping Him with all of their hearts. It was a foreign thing to me. Brought up in the Catholic Church and then brought to Christ in the Baptist church in my early adulthood I had never experienced anything like it. It was very different from what I was used to. I began to try and do what I saw so I raised my hands like everybody else, but something was missing. I would look around at all of the serene faces, worshipping God and I wondered why I wasn't getting that. I would go up for prayer at the end of a service and watch person after person fall under the power of the spirit and I would wonder why I felt little to nothing when I was prayed for.

When I received Inner Healing & Deliverance I discovered that I had a slumbering spirit. It wasn't that God wasn't moving it was simply that my personal spirit wasn't awakened to what was going on around it.

How do we recognize this condition?

When there is little or no strength of character in certain areas of life, a slumbering spirit can be present. For example, if a person struggles with lying and repents for this, but then continues to lie repeatedly, a slumbering spirit may be suspect.

People with slumbering spirits can be born-again, spirit-filled, Bible-believing, and church going. They may even be serving in the ministry. It is not about their abilities – it is about their inability to help themselves.

Identifying a Slumbering Spirit

It is in the following eight areas that the slumbering spirit cannot operate. Use this list (from *Healing the Wounded Spirit* by John and Paula Sandford) to determine whether you are dealing with a client whose spirit slumbers.

1. Corporate worship   *I Corinthians 2:14*
Awakened personal spirits sense the presence of God. Slumbering spirits can only *believe* God is present.

2. Private devotion with God   *Job 32:8*

Awakened personal spirits can be with God and feel His love. For those with slumbering spirits, devotionals and the Word run dry.

3. Hearing revelations from God
Slumbering spirits have difficulty listening and hearing revelation from God. Awakened personal spirits have spiritual dreams, see visions and hear from the Lord.

4. Maintaining health *Proverbs 17:22; 18:14*
An awakened person quickly recovers from illness; if the condition is serious or terminal, the spirit can still thrive. Those with slumbering spirits heal slowly and despair when illness strikes.

5. Original insight and inspiration is not uncommon to the awakened spirit. These individuals are inspired to creative acts. Those with slumbering spirits tend to mimic, rather than to create. One person goes to art school and graduates, yet when they paint or draw, the picture appears flat and uninspiring. The awakened one graduates from the same school and paints a picture that moves the soul.

6. The ability to relate to time, past, present, and future is the capability of the awakened spirit. They can remember good times as well as bad. However, those with slumbering spirits have a tendency to be confined to the pain of the moment. The couples with a struggling marriage that have awakened spirits can remember the joy that they once experienced, and this gives them hope for the future. The couples with the slumbering spirits are confined to the pain of the moment; they cannot muster the hope to see beyond the immediate problem.

7. Empathetic communication is that ability to sense the meaning behind the words of another. An awakened spirit has this ability, where the person with the slumbering spirit can track only with the mind.

The wife has worked hard all day. The children have worried her last nerve; she is exhausted and needs a break. Her husband comes home from work feels compassion for his wife and he says, "come on, I'll call the babysitter, and you and I will go out, have a nice quiet dinner and you can relax." The wife thinking about the budget and knowing that he worked hard as well says, "That's alright honey we probably can't afford that expense." The man with the slumbering spirit says, "Well OK dear, we can stay home if that's what you want." *He heard her words, but not her spirit!* He can only track with his mind. If his spirit were awake, he would have heard her spirit say, *"I'm trying to be considerate, but I would really love a break."* People with a slumbering spirit have a very difficult time sustaining relationships, due to the fact that they cannot hear the spirit of their mate, they can only track the words.

8. Mature conscience *I John 3:9*

There is a vast difference between repentance and remorse. Repentance from the Greek metanoeo, means "to change one's mind and purpose, as the result of after knowledge." Remorse on the other hand is "a feeling of deep regret"

Awakened Christians possess a true conscience, which works powerfully before the event, warning them from sinning against God and their fellow man. Those with slumbering spirits have only remorse conscience. They become angry for the sin that they committed, but are not truly repentant. They do not want to be confronted with it, nor do they want to be reminded of it. "I'm over it! Why aren't you?"

How can a Born again Believer's spirit slumber?

Either through a lack of affection, attention, and appropriate touch or as a result of wounding.

Children need plenty of wholesome and affectionate love, and the parent is the vessel that is supposed to provide it. Parents need to draw the spirit forward unto life, as well as to provide boundaries through appropriate discipline. They are commissioned by God to build strength of character into a child through example and modeling. If they raise a child in the way he should go, a true conscience will be developed. While it is the mothers who give birth to the child, it is the Fathers responsibility to call a child's spirit to life.

Even if the child was shown nurture and care by both parents, it is possible for a person to 'shut down' because of traumatic incidents that caused the spirit of the believer to shut itself off and thereby, over time, slumber. False teaching in the church can cause the believer to resist the gifts and callings of God which causes their personal spirit to 'check out.' The spirit needs to be called back to life and alertness.

Captive Spirit

"The thief comes to steal, kill and destroy; I have come that they may have life, and have it to the full." --John 10:10

This is a condition that occurs when an individual who has been wounded turns away from life, or becomes spiritually rebellious. We lock our selves in fleshly strongholds, unable to function; often demons take advantage.

Rather than being wakened to life, captive or imprisoned spirits must be set free from powers of darkness. The gifts of knowledge and discernment are needed and a careful observation of the symptoms plaguing the individual is required.

A slumbering spirit does not know that it slumbers, but a captive spirit knows that there is more or that they possess gifts and talents that are not being realized. They don't know why they can't make it happen. There is frustration and torment associated with a captive spirit.

When I ask clients, "Do you feel there is greatness in you? A better version of yourself inside that just can't seem to break free?" I only get two answers, the first is a blank stare followed closely with a noooo. The second is an emphatic YES and this pleading look of hope that says, "Do you see it too!" In this second case the client's spirit is most definitely held captive. Such was the case with Dwayne.

Dwayne came to see me, struggling, with inferiority issues. He always felt he could do better then he was doing. He couldn't understand why he couldn't get in touch with the greatness inside him. He knew he was in there and he could feel it. He used the analogy of Superman forever being trapped in Clark Kent. He was the mild mannered geeky guy that got picked on and ridiculed. Unfortunately he couldn't just change into Superman and save the day. It was as if Superman were imprisoned.

I explained to Dwayne who he truly was became imprisoned and that he suffered from a captive spirit. I asked Dwayne if he had ever put a jigsaw puzzle together. He allowed that he had. I asked him, "You know how when you put a puzzle together, no matter how beautiful the picture is if a piece is missing the picture is simple incomplete?" He agreed. "The enemy has stolen a piece of your puzzle." I continued, "But the Lord is going to retrieve it." When we prayed for the Lord to retrieve the missing piece, to open the door to the captive, I saw the change in the young man. He sat straighter, He was more confident. A courage he had never known rose up in him to face life's challenges and upsets. The captive had been set free.

Origins of Captivity

Most captivity begins in the womb, or infancy, but sometimes in later childhood and even adulthood. Older children have ways of coping without detaching from life. They express feelings verbally, draw boundaries, or even fight back. Infants, however, can only react to abuse or neglect by refusing to bond, or by "disconnecting". This disconnecting can become a practiced response. Final healing usually comes after a series of "reconnections". The client must repent for detaching from life. Look for inner vows not to feel, not to need, not to express, and not to be. The absolute extreme to the disconnecting could result in multiple personalities (Now known as Dis-associative disorder.)

Depression

"Like one who takes away a garment on a cold day, or like vinegar poured on soda, is one who sings songs to a heavy heart." --Prov 25:20

Depression is one of the most prevalent and insidious disorders of our lifetime. Nearly 15% of the populations of developed countries suffer from some form of depression. The fastest growing population for depression is children growing at a rate of 23% According to Psychologist Dr. Bob Murray of the Uplift Program.

What is Depression?

Depression is a condition in which the personal spirit has lost its capacity to function in terms of its ability to supply energy for life. Depression is not a sign of weakness, a lack of faith, or the result of negative thinking. It's like turning the knob of a stove top on, but nothing happens.

Depression vs. Despondency

We all experience despondency from time to time. This is not the same as true depression. The despondent person knows that there are things that will help, i.e., music, exercise, friends, etc. This person still has hope for better times. They still have some confidence in self: "I will be able to do it tomorrow." They are only affected emotionally, and psychologically.

The depressed person on the other hand is sure that nothing will help. They are convinced that tomorrow will be as black as today, and they have lost all hope. They are certain that they cannot be fixed. This person is affected chemically and physically, as well as psychologically.

Some degree of chemical imbalance is common in true depression. Ministers should not countermand prescribed medication. If a client asks you if they should stop taking their medication, simply tell them to continue to go to their physician. As the physician sees their improvement the doctor will decrease the medication.

How to recognize depression

The client will tell you that they are depressed. You are to believe them. Their behavior will be a good indication, such as withdrawal, general listlessness, and the inability to take teasing, or handle pressure of any kind. Any challenge, criticism, or workload no matter how light will overwhelm the clinically depressed. Their appearance will be an indication as well i.e., eyes dull and lack life, and hair has no luster, shoulders may be sagging.

Many of the things we can say or do to help a despondent person should not be done for one who is depressed. Don't tell them to cheer up, or get over it. Parties and celebrations will do more to depress them than to make them feel better. Suggesting that they go to a comedy club, ballgame, or concert will tend to re-enforce how bad off they really are. Because they won't be moved to laughter or excitement they will slip deeper into depression as they watch everyone else having fun. They know something is dreadfully wrong with them. Trying to build their faith and understanding by preaching or teaching, giving advice (self-help books, diets, exercises, or time management tips) taking them to prayer meetings, worship services, or asking them to begin private devotionals often makes things worse.

Root causes of depression are:

- Failure to "earn" love. Performance Orientation will lead to discouragement and ultimately to depression.
- Silent anger/rage turned inward.
- Hidden guilt and shame
- Inability to forgive self, and others
- Childhood wounds either sexual or physical repressed or forgotten.
- Deprivation of affection.
- Early loss by divorce or separation, abandonment, adoption, or death.
- Judgments
- Prenatal and birth trauma. Being a "replacement child."
- Loss of job, retirement, drastic changes
- Death of mate or divorce
- Physical/psychic trauma such as postpartum experience, loss of limb, or hysterectomy.
- Sustained travel
- Chemical imbalance

The following is a list of don'ts for one on one ministering:

- Don't smile too much
- Don't stand while the other sits
- Don't invade personal space
- Don't minister in close quarters (small room with doors closed)
- Don't appear unconfident about ability to help. Be confident in the Lord.
- Don't let them measure success or failure by emotions or feelings.
- Don't pray, "If it be Thy will." God's will is to heal them!
- Don't say, "You can or I can show you how." Any effort on their part will seem insurmountable.
- Don't ask person to make a decision about the next appointment, simply state "I want to see you next…"

Healing for depression:

- Weep with them *Romans 12:15*
- Validate their feelings by sharing words that give a picture of where they are i.e., I understand that things look black; I understand that you have no energy; I realize that you can't stand people; you feel guilty, everyone says cheer up; you feel as though it's impossible; you feel like tomorrow will be as black as today, etc. This lets them know that you truly understand how they feel and this will help build their confidence in you.
- Express confidence. Tell them that you know exactly what to do and that "they will be healed." *Luke 5:17* "Let them know that they don't have to have faith." *Romans 3:3*
- Pray simply and vividly.
- Make specific dates to meet them, and always keep appointments.
- Note changes, affirm, and compliment. Do not give false complements, and don't over compliment.
- Encourage them to begin to do things they like.
- Maintain relationship
- Don't judge what you hear.

NOTE: If you are seeing someone that you feel is clinically depressed refer the client to a physician and work together. Find a Christian Psychiatrist who is willing to work with you.

Recommended Questions:

Slumbering Spirit:
- Do you find yourself standing in worship wondering why everyone around you is receiving but not you?
- Do you take a long time to recover from illnesses?
- Do you have a hard time entering into the things of God?

Captive Spirit:
- Do you feel there is greatness in you that can't seem to bust out?
- Do you feel like there is a better version of you in there somewhere?
- Do you have any phobias, or deep rooted fears (dark, close spaces, snakes, heights, etc)?

Depression:
- Do you struggle with depression?
- Does it feel like it will never get better? (discerning between depression & Despondency)

Sample Prayers:

Slumbering Spirit:

Have Client Repeat: "Lord, I recognize my spirit is not fully functional, not fully awake in several areas. For some reason (*confess if known*) my spirit chose not to enter into life. I confess this as sin; I have put my light under a bushel. Like Jonah, I have fled from the life you designed for me. And, as with Jonah, my refusal to live in these areas has caused trouble. I ask your forgiveness for the ways I have wounded those around me Lord. I ask your forgiveness for being unwilling to live life."

Spoken over Client: "As you have confessed and repented for not engaging in life I speak the forgiveness of Almighty God over you. I say you are forgiven. The Lord is washing your sin into the Sea of Forgetfulness where He remembers it no more."

Have Client Repeat: "Father I ask you to awaken my spirit. Cleanse my spirit and remove the cobwebs. I choose life. I choose to be present and I choose to engage. Bring to death Lord that impulse to hide and to flee. Help me to see your call to life as a loving call. Help me to see the call of those who love me in the same way. Open my ears Lord that I might hear your call and the call of my loved ones. In Jesus Name."

Spoken over Client: "Lord I thank you for opening (**client's**) ears so they may hear your call to life. I thank you that you are giving them courage to stand in adversity. (**Client**) I call your slumbering spirit to awaken in Jesus Holy Name."

Captive Spirit:

Have Client Repeat: "Father I am not complete. The enemy has stolen that which is mine. He has taken my spirit captive and has left me bound in fear (*specific from interview*). Father I ask you to free my spirit and return it to me. Take back what the enemy has stolen and restore the years. Make me whole in Jesus Holy name."

Spoken over Client: "The Lord is not hindered by time or space. Right now he is going to that prison (*use specific fears from interview*) and he is unlocking your prison door. He is taking you by the hand and he is leading you out of darkness into His glorious light. The Lord is knitting your spirit together with your soul and body and He is making you every whit whole in Jesus holy name."

Depression:

Spoken over Client: "Father I ask you to come into the darkness that is (**Client's**) life right now. All energies, spiritual, emotional, and physical are used up. Lord they have called out to You and heard no answer. Nothing changed.

I ask you Lord to come and rekindle the flame of (**Client's**) spirit. Little by little, and at a pace they can bear. Increase your light and energize their spirit. Jesus come and let the warmth of Your presence flow from the center of his being outward. He may not feel any immediate difference. That's okay. I know, Lord, in time, the good feelings will come.

Father I ask that you bless (**Client's**) sleep so that rest reaches deep into the exhaustion. Begin the renewal process in Jesus Holy Name.

(There is no prayer of repentance for depression. The client truly suffering from this is not in a place to repent. Healing is required before the client can turn the eye inward to find those areas where repentance is needed.)

Chapter 11: Prayers of Deliverance (Uncommon)

Burden Bearing

"Brothers, if someone is caught in a sin, you who are spiritual should restore him gently. But watch yourself, or you also may be tempted. Carry each other's burdens, and in this way you will fulfill the law of Christ....Each one should test his own actions. Then he can take pride in himself, without comparing himself to somebody else, for each one should carry his own load." --Gal 6:1,2,4 NIV

A Burden Bearer is one who empathizes with and takes upon themselves the problems of another. Intercessors, prayer warriors, counselors, mental heath professionals, even good listening friends all are examples of burden bearers. The carrying of others burdens is scriptural as seen in Galatians. But there is a right and a wrong way to do this. Burden bearers who carry their families, friends, co-workers and others problems around with them daily, letting these problems effect their emotions and flesh, or are trying to fix these loved ones, find themselves mentally, emotionally, and physically exhausted from all of their labors. To these, what was given as a gift at conception has become a curse. The yoke of burden they carry around with them gets heavier and heavier until they collapse under the weight of it. When burden bearing is done rightly we hear the problem and immediately begin to pray (even if only within our spirits) taking the burden to the cross and giving it to Almighty God. We then leave it with Him believing that, *"whatever things you ask when you pray, believe that you receive them, and you will have them." (Mark 11:24 NKJV)*

When I was a Youth Pastor at a small fellowship in Powder Springs, GA I taught my group about the difference between rightly and wrongly carrying another's burdens. I had my ten teenagers each close and pick up their metal folding chairs. I told them to hold them at arms length until they couldn't any longer. As the first of them began to weaken I rushed over and said,"Here that looks heavy let me take it for you." taking her chair along with my own. I continued from student to student collecting chairs as they would start to drop until I was holding nine of the student's chairs along with my own.

With five folding chairs in each arm I shared how by taking their burdens I may have made life easier for them but I was so bogged down under the weight of them I could barely move, much less help anyone else. I explained that the only way I was going to free myself was to take the burdens I was carrying and "Hurl them to the foot of the cross." With that I tossed all ten chairs toward the platform.

Calmly I walked to the one remaining student still stubbornly holding onto her chair. "You see," I explained, "when we carry burdens in our flesh or emotions we get bogged down. However," I held out my hands to accept the young girl's chair, "If we carry the burden in our spirit, praying for the need," I turned toward the pile of chairs at the platform, "and then take them to the cross," I tossed the last chair on the pile, "Then we are carrying them rightly. We are only to carry the burdens *God* gives us; we carry them *in* our spirits, and *only* as far as the cross."

"For My yoke is easy and My burden is light." –Matt 11:30 (NKJV)

"Most assuredly, I say to you, the Son can do nothing of Himself, but what He sees the Father do; for whatever He does, the Son also does in like manner." –John 5:19 (NKJV)

The need is not the call. Jesus only said what the Father told him to say and only did what the Father told him to do. Jesus walked by the lame man at the Gate Beautiful any time he went to the temple in Jerusalem to teach or pray. The man would have been there begging for alms much like he was in Acts 3:5 when Peter and John came upon him. Despite his begging and obvious *need* Jesus did not heal him. Why? Because it was Peter's call for the building of his faith and for God's glory.

Each of us is surrounded by our own needs, or those of others, but we must remember that *we* are not able to meet all of them. We must remember that, "...*God shall supply all of [your] need according to His riches in glory by Christ Jesus.*" (Phil 4:19) If we are trying to meet every need, we will become "weary in well doing" and collapse under the weight of everyone's burden. This puts us exactly where the enemy wants us - ineffective and essentially out of the battle. When we allow the Lord to direct us in our burden bearing it becomes a blessing instead of a curse. We become a precision instrument that the Lord can use to perform surgery on the wounded.

How do we let the Lord direct us in our burden bearing? We begin by understanding that we are not the savior to all, Jesus is. We cannot meet every need all the time and there are others who will do their part to meet it as well. Next we must listen to Him. The Lord will quicken your spirit to the need before you if it is yours to carry. Finally we do *only* what we are called to do. If we are called to pray we pray, if we are to give we give (only what we are told to give), etc. When we do this we can walk away from the situation knowing that we have done what the Lord has asked us and we can trust that He will continue the work to its completion. We are now free to meet the next need he calls us to.

Empathetic Defilement

This occurs when, in the process of identifying with others and bearing their burdens, our mind and or/heart translates their problems as our own. Burden bearing is not defilement; it is simply feeling what others feel. As we identify with these feelings they are drawn through us and are to be left at the cross. We become defiled when our minds and/or hearts embrace the lie that what we are feeling originates from us. In the areas of relationship and sexuality, defilement can speed the progression of spiritual adultery into physical adultery.

"...There is nothing outside the man which going into him can defile him; but the things which proceed out of the man are what defile the man." Mark 7:15

PDMs need to be careful to guard their hearts and not become too involved with the client. A discerning PDM can feel the sexual desires of a client and misinterpret it as originating from them instead of the client. If there is an open door in the PDM they could fall into a compromising situation, and see their ministry destroyed.

Not all empathetic defilement is related to spiritual adultery. A doctor, sensing a mother's helplessness at seeing her child sick, begins to feel helpless himself. Of course this is not the case, what has happened is he has experienced her emotions. Many times we can recognize when we are burden bearing for another, but sometimes our hearts and minds become deceived when we appropriate their feeling onto ourselves. Unhealed areas in our lives can open doorways for the enemy to deceive us and confuse us. The PDM needs to be aware and keep their hearts pure.

Discerning Empathetic Defilement

Very often, the feelings and thoughts don't fit, as in the example of the doctor, or those feelings come out of left field somewhere. However, if you think that they could fit, and discernment isn't clear, consider the following safeguards:

- Never act hastily. Give the Holy Spirit time to clear confusion and restore clarity.
- Talk with close friends and spouse, without breaking any confidence.
- Pray cleansing prayers over yourself.
- Ask the Lord for sharper discernment; learn from experience, and maintain safe boundaries.
- Understand the problem: "For wisdom is protection...wisdom preserves the lives of its possessors." Ecclesiastes 7:12

Occult Involvement

"There shall not be found among you anyone who makes his son or his daughter pass through the fire, or one who practices witchcraft, or a soothsayer, or one who interprets omens, or a sorcerer, or one who conjures spells, or a medium, or a spiritist, or one who calls up the dead."—Deut 18:10-11 (NKJV)

"For rebellion is as the sin of witchcraft, and stubbornness is as iniquity and idolatry."
--1Sam 15:23 (NKJV)

"For God's gifts and His call are irrevocable. [He never withdraws them when once they are given, and He does not change His mind about those to whom He gives His grace or to whom He sends His call.]" –Rom 11:29 (AMP)

God gives all of his children spiritual gifts. Given at conception these gifts are not contingent on how we choose to use them. Every spiritual gift spoken of in the Word of God is active and in use today whether or not we choose to believe in them. Unfortunately because of faulty church doctrine and teaching many who are hungry for something real are turning to 'spirituality,' new age, and other occult practices.

I myself left the church when I was twelve years old in search of something *real*. As I sat in another lifeless and dull church service trying to stay awake I said to myself, "There has to be more to it than this!" I didn't know what the 'more to it' was but I was determined to find out. Unfortunately I had no real spiritual guidance and I quickly found myself drawn to the occult. The realm of the supernatural *is* real and demonic forces are willing to submit for a time playing along and drawing the unwitting victim deeper and deeper. The deception is that the victims think they are in control, when in fact they are not.

By the time I was seventeen I was thoroughly entrenched. I led séances, summoned the dead, cast spells, would spiritually travel outside my body (called astral projection); I could interpret dreams and empathetically heal the sick. Basically I was actively doing everything warned against in Deuteronomy 18:10-11. Worst of all I was completely deceived into thinking that I was absolutely in control of the forces I was employing. Do not be fooled there are *only* two sources from which to draw spiritually – God or Satan.

On one occasion, I was awakened in the middle of the night by *something*. There was a distinct absence of light, and it was freezing cold. A terror gripped me that I had never known in my life. Without thinking, my hand shot out and hit a Bible I had placed on the nightstand earlier, and before I even knew what I was saying I heard the words coming out of my mouth, "In the name of Jesus all evil spirits be gone from this place!" In an instant I felt a peace I had never experienced flood my body. My eyes, which had been forced shut from terror now opened and I could see the familiar outlines of furniture in the dark, the LED lights on my stereo across the room, etc. The next morning I found three marks on the paneling above my bed right over where my head was laid the night before resembling claw marks. This experience changed me.

The supernatural world is every bit as real as this one. There are forces that are not to be trifled with. This is why the Lord forbids these practices. He is our refuge and our strength. He alone is a strong tower we can run into and be safe. He is our Heavenly Father who is looking out for our well being.

"He gave them power over unclean spirits, to cast them out," –Matt 10:1 (NKJV)

"Deaf and dumb spirit, I command you, come out of him and enter him no more!"
–Mark 9:25 (NKJV)

We are given authority in the name of Jesus to cast out unclean spirits. We are to cast them out commanding them to "enter no more," and then inviting the Holy Spirit to take up residence filling the void these spirits have left. This is our *only* involvement with the occult - driving out unclean spirits.

Examples of Occult practices:

- Mysticism, Séances, Ouija Boards, Tarot Cards, Palm Reading
- New Age, Crystals, Pyramids…
- Spiritualism, Astral Projection, etc.
- Sorcery, illusion, telekinesis, telepathy
- Satanic Cults, animal sacrifice, sexual rituals, etc.

All dealings with the occult must be repented of and renounced. All misuse of spiritual gifts must be repented of. Ask the Lord to retrain them in the proper use of these gifts. For those who no longer want the gifts God has given them it is important to explain that these gifts were given them to help them spread the Kingdom of God. They are precious and should not be thrown away. To do so is to say we know better than God and *is* spiritual rebellion.

Physical Disease

"And Jesus went about all Galilee, teaching in their synagogues, preaching the gospel of the kingdom, and healing **all** *kinds of sickness and* **all** *kinds of disease among the people."* --Matt 4:23 (NKJV)

"But He was wounded for our transgressions, He was bruised for our iniquities; The chastisement for our peace was upon Him, And by His stripes we are healed."
—Isa 53:5 (NKJV)

Disease comes in many forms. No matter the form the origin remains the same. Disease starts in the spirit, moves into our souls and eventually affects our bodies. While there are far too many forms of disease to name here, Pastor Henry Wright catalogues many of them in his book "A More Excellent Way." I use it when searching out the spiritual roots of diseases / illnesses that my clients are afflicted with. I have had great success with it. In his book, every disease named stems from one of thirty-nine root diseases. The exact number of stripes Jesus took for our healing. Everything Jesus did was with a purpose in mind. Isaiah prophesied our healing was going to come through the lashings that Jesus took.

Praying for physical healing for clients can be daunting. What if it doesn't work? This question can loom over us even as we pray. Here is something that will help. *THE NEED IS NOT THE CALL!* You must remember this. Remember the example given in the burden bearing section about the lame man's healing? It was for Peter and John to fulfill, not Jesus. If someone comes to you asking for prayer, pray, but pray understanding that your responsibility ends there. It is God who heals not us. It is imperative to learn not to take credit for those that are set free, nor to take blame for those that are not. Our obedience to God is the important thing, praying when we are told to and believing at all times.

Healing is God's will. It is part of salvation. Salvation isn't only about going to Heaven when we die. It is about how we are living today. Salvation encompasses healing, freedom, relationship, redemption, renewal, and wholeness.

Recommended Questions:

Burden Bearing

- Do you feel like you need to help others?
- Do you find yourself empathizing with their pain?
- Do friends, family, etc. often unload their troubles on you?
- Do you feel like there is no one else who can / will help so you must?

Occult Involvement

- Have you ever been involved in the occult?
- Have you ever been to a psychic?
- Have you ever played with a Ouija board, tarot cards, rune stones or the like?
- Did you have any invisible playmates as a child?
- Where you or any member of your family part of the Masons, or Eastern Star?
- Where you or any member of your family part of Wicca, druids, or in any way involved in witchcraft?
- Have you been part of 'fringe Christian' groups like Latter Day Saints or Jehovah's Witness?

Physical Disease

(These should be ascertained when making the appointment preferably so adequate preparation can be made.)

- What diseases run through your family lineage?
- Are you feeling any pains in your body right now?
- What diseases have you been diagnosed with?

Sample Prayers

Burden Bearing

Have Client Repeat: "Heavenly Father you gave me this gift of Burden Bearing. But this gift has become a curse. I confess I have carried everyone's burdens. I have carried them in my flesh and in my emotions and they have overwhelmed me. I repent for misusing this gift and for not trusting in you. Father I take all of these burdens and I hurl them to the foot of your cross along with the yoke of burden bearing. Father, teach me how to use this gift for your glory in Jesus Holy name."

Spoken over Client: "As you have confessed and repented for carrying burdens that were not yours and for carrying them wrongly, in your flesh and your emotions, I speak the forgiveness of Almighty God over you. He is washing these burdens from you and cleansing you from all defilement. He is breaking the yoke of burden bearing from off of your shoulders. You will now only carry the burdens He gives you. You will carry them only in the spirit and only as far as his cross as He intended. For His burden is light and His yoke is easy.

Father I thank you that you are taking this gift from **Client** and you are redefining it. Father you are giving it back to them with understanding that they need *only* carry the burdens you give them and then *only* as far as your cross. Father they are not to let these burdens get into their emotions or effect their flesh but they will carry them *only* in their spirits as you intend in Jesus holy name."

Occult Involvement

Have Client Repeat: "Father your word forbids us from seeking after the occult. I confess and repent that I have done that which is forbidden (Have client repent for specifics from interview). I repent for any participation I have had with the occult, Baal worship, witchcraft and spiritual assignments. I thank you Lord for breaking them off of me and off of my bloodline. Lord please reap all that I have sown."

Spoken over Client: "God is severing off your bloodline every disease, every sin, every curse, and every form of addiction, every form of witchcraft, or spiritual assignment in Jesus Holy Name.

The Lord is taking His severe sword (from Isaiah 27:1) and is severing the bonds that you made with: (list the things they bonded with)."

Any bonding with: Baal Worship (mixing sexual perversion with worship)

Poverty	Familiar spirits
Infirmity	Jealousy
Addictions	Voodoo
Pornography	Witchcraft
Envy	homosexuality
Etc.	

Have Client Repeat: "Father, I repent for bonding with any of these curses, sins, addictions or spiritual assignments. I thank you Lord for my deliverance."

Physical Disease

(Because the spiritual roots of diseases are wide and varied I suggest researching them in "A More Excellent Way" By Pastor Henry Wright. Lead the client in repentance and forgiveness in the areas necessary and speak forgiveness and healing over them in the name of Jesus.)

Chapter 12: Deliverance, The Casting Away of Unclean Spirits.

"When angry, do not sin; do not ever let your wrath (your exasperation, your fury or indignation) last until the sun goes down. Leave no [such] room or foothold for the devil [give no opportunity to him]." –Eph 4:26-27

As mentioned in the introduction of this guide many Christians object to the idea that a Christian can be demon-possessed, because possession implies ownership. Since Scripture states, *"You are not your own; you were bought with a price" I Corinthians 6:19-20* their question is, how can there be dual ownership? The answer is, there can't be dual ownership. A Christian cannot be possessed as we think of possession as in "The Exorcist." The concept of this type of possession although Biblical is very rare and almost always involves non-believers. More common to believer and non-believer alike however is affliction by a demon / unclean spirit. This occurs when we leave a door open for the enemy to come and torment us.

The word "possession" is found in neither the Greek, nor Hebrew text. The following 3 terms are used to describe this condition.

- To "Have a demon" Matthew 11:18; Luke 8:27
- To "be in a demon" Mark 1:23; 5:2
- To "be demonized" from the Greek daimonidzomai, the word most commonly translated as "possessed" Mark 1:32; Luke 8:36. Is literally, "to be bothered by a demon"

There are still some Christians who believe that Scripture refutes the possibility of demons in our lives. *"If anyone is in Christ, he is a new creation, the old has gone, the new has come."* II Corinthians 5:17. This is however, truncated, incomplete theology, because we still sin.

"If we say we have no sin [refusing to admit that we are sinners], we delude and lead ourselves astray, and the Truth [which the Gospel presents] is not in us [does not dwell in our hearts]."--1 John 1:8 (AMP)

Spirits can afflict or "demonize" us in any area where sin persists in our lives. Where there is unforgiveness, there is an opportunity for spirits to dwell and influence us. Because a demon afflicts rather than possesses us, our choices are the determining factor in allowing demons access into our lives. In every case in the New Testament where a reason is given for demonization, the occurrence is preceded by a choice to sin. (James 4:7; Acts 5:1; I Corinthians 5:5; II timothy 2:25-26.)

Open Doors to the Enemy

Demons specialize in various areas of human nature and enter through doors we open by sin and judgment to torment us through:
- Physical violation, Mark 2-5
- Illness and infirmity, Matthew 17:15-18; Mark 9:17-27; Luke 13:11-13
- Sexual problems, Mark 16:9; Luke 8:2; I Corinthians 6:18
- Mental Deception, Acts 5:2-3; 16:16; I Timothy 4:1
- Emotional Turmoil, I Samuel 16:14; Matthew 8; Mark 5; Luke 8
- Relationship troubles, Judges 9:23
- Involvement in occult, spiritual sins Deuteronomy 18:9-13; Leviticus 20:27; Acts 13:1-13; 16:16-18

Our sin, judgments, etc. are like open doors that allow the enemy access to our lives physically, emotionally, and spiritually. Once these sins, judgments, etc. are confessed and repented of, then those doors of access can be shut to the enemy.

Levels of Demonic Influence

- <u>Oppression:</u> Demons are all around the person, not inhabiting, but able to reach in to influence and temporarily control whenever the person indulges in sinful thoughts and actions.
- <u>Infiltration:</u> In those areas of our lives where Jesus is not - anything else can be. Jesus isn't where pride, anger, unforgiveness, immorality, offense, bitterness, hate, vain imaginings, thrive and abide. When we receive these into our minds and hearts we also receive the spiritual influence that accompanies them. Some might protest that these are emotions and feelings, and they would be

right, but it is also true that they have accompanying spirits. However, we have found that they are invited in by virtue of the open door to the sinful behavior.

- <u>Obsession</u>: This is a psychological and spiritual term/condition. A habit in the flesh is sometimes compulsive, and serves as a house for demonic torment. These habits, patterns, and structures influence and encourage the demonic activity and are the core of the obsession.
- <u>Possession</u>: In this condition, the original character and personality of the person are entirely suppressed; demons are in full control. Possession is extremely rare, except in some non-Christian countries.

True possession would be the exception to my rule that we do not cast evil spirits out of anyone. I would cast them out and then see if the person was interested in keeping them out. To be possessed would mean that the person would have no free will, but rather the will of that person was taken away by demonic force. We then being the strong one (because of the power of the Holy Spirit in us) would cleanse that house and give the person the freewill to choose.

Healing Begins with Relationship

We cannot overemphasize the importance of relationship in ministering to others. Relationship is something Jesus wants with us that He does not want with demons. For this reason, He always silenced demons, but never their victims.

Healing begins by establishing relationship, and ends in restored relationships. When Jesus met a man whose demonized son suffered epileptic fits, He could have chosen to cast it out immediately. Instead, He spoke with the man about faith, and soon the man was asking the Lord to help him in his unbelief. It was only after this that Jesus cast the spirit out of the boy.

Thus the father found a relationship with God who asks for faithfulness, yet sympathizes with our weaknesses and wants to come close to us. Through this, both father and son were healed and delivered.

Satan is an expert at subterfuge. He burrows into the soft tissue of our souls, i.e., bitter root judgments, and inner vows. The termite effect is when he moves from his entrance point into other rebellions or sinful character structures in us. Therefore the client may have to be delivered from demons which have little to do with what symptoms they are presenting. A woman may suffer from a spirit of rage against boys and men, but this may have opened a door for a spirit of defiance against all authority, or there may be a spirit of condemnation that keeps her from being able to accept any compliment. Allow the Holy Spirit to lead you in all these areas. Both deliverance and inner healing must be accomplished in most circumstances.

Leaving No Foothold

"When an unclean spirit goes out of a man, he goes through dry places, seeking rest, and finds none. Then he says, 'I will return to my house from which I came.' And when he comes, he finds it empty, swept, and put in order. Then he goes and takes with him seven other spirits more wicked than himself, and they enter and dwell there; and the last state of that man is worse than the first. So shall it also be with this wicked generation."
--Matt 12:43-45 (NKJV)

It is imperative that when an unclean spirit is cast out that the Holy Spirit be invited to fill the empty vessel. In the above scripture the spirit wasn't inherently cast out but the result is the same. The man is worse off. Once an unclean spirit is cast out it is necessary to invite the Holy Spirit to fill the void the evil spirit has left. Then loose the Key of David to shut any doors the enemy has used to gain access, for what He shuts no one may open and what He opens no one shuts. Ask the Lord to blind the enemy as He did at Sodom so the enemy can't even find an entrance into the client.

Cautions regarding a deliverance session

- Do not command demons to name themselves.
- Do not converse with or curse demons.
- Do not seek or require any manifestations.
- Do not idolize methods; instead, respond according to the needs and condition of the client.

If you have a Baptist sitting in front of you and you start to jump up and down screaming in tongues, your client may have a heart attack! You will have cast that demon out, but your patient has died. (That may be a slight exaggeration, but I think you get the picture.)

Demons don't respond to the volume of your voice, they respond to the power that is in the name of Jesus Christ. Whispering the name of Jesus with power and authority will echo into the spiritual world louder than any screaming out of methodology.

Bringing Healing to the Oppressed

Instruct client on how to maintain their healing. Healing and deliverance start in the spirit, flow into the soul and then affect the body. Repentance, confession, and forgiveness is the way to cleanse, humility is the secret to maintaining the cleansing. If we choose not to take offense we open the door for the Lord to fight our battles, and give Satan no opening for any demonic oppression in our lives.

Recommended Questions:

The unclean spirits at work in the client's life will be revealed throughout the interview process. Pay special attention to these questions but let the Holy Spirit lead you throughout the interview.

- What brings you to see me today?
- If you could change one thing about your spouse, what would it be? What's the one thing your spouse would change about you?
- How do you get along with your children?
- Do you ever feel as though you don't fit in anywhere? (Orphan Spirit)
- Do you feel as though there is greatness inside of you that can't get out? (captive spirit)
- Do you find that you often sabotage yourself?
- What kind of personality did your dad have? How about your mom?
- Did you have any invisible friends as a child? Do you remember their names? (familiar spirits)
- Any difficult or traumatic incidents in your childhood that trouble you now?
- Is there anything that you know God has forgiven you for, but are finding it hard to forgive yourself? (Shame, Blame Guilt)

Sample Prayers:

Review interview sheet and have client cast evil spirits into outer darkness. (Let the Holy Spirit lead):

Have Client Repeat: "As an act of my will and by the authority of Jesus Christ I cast far from me the spirit of _____ (list & repeat) never to return. Heavenly Father, send your Holy Spirit and fill the void where these evil spirits have left. Fill me to overflowing with your peace, joy, life, and light.

Spirits of:

Despair	division	unforgiveness
Rejection	loneliness	separation
Jealousy	lying spirit	isolation
Detachment	envy	deception
Intimidation	confusion	pride
Lust	Religious	confounding
Rebellion	anger	rage
Fear	inadequacy	sabotage
Self-abuse	depression	Incompletion
Deaf & dumb	abandonment	inconsolable
Sadness	Molech	low self-esteem
Low self-worth	Invalidation	invisibility
Incubus/Succubus	Sexually Perverse	

Spoken over Client: "Now I come into agreement with you... casting these evil spirits far from you *never* to return. Heavenly Father, send your Holy spirit to fill every void that every evil spirit has left with Your life and light."

"The Holy Spirit is rising within you like a fountain of living water rising up out of your belly. As it rises within you it is enveloping your heart, eroding and washing away your walls of stone. The Holy Spirit is replacing your heart of stone with the heart of our Lord and Savior Jesus. He is causing your heart to beat in time with his own so when you place your hand on your chest it is no longer your heartbeat you are feeling but his. As he continues rising within you he is cleansing your mind. He is scouring the three levels of your mind; the conscious, subconscious, even unconscious. He is renewing your mind; giving you the mind of Christ.

Now just as a glass filled to overflowing so the water of the Holy Spirit is spilling out of the crown of your head and flowing down, covering your ears, so that he is washing the blockages from your ears. Every word spoken to you will now be filtered by the Holy Spirit and you will no longer hear the word but the spirit by which the word was spoken. You will hear the Lord more clearly than ever before. As the Holy Spirit flows over your eyes He is washing the scales from your eyes. You will no longer see people after the flesh but according to the Spirit. The Lord is opening your spiritual eyes to see. He continues pouring down over your lips and every word you speak will be filtered by the Holy Spirit. Others will no longer misunderstand your words because they are filtered by Almighty God.

As he flows down over your shoulders he is washing away every burden you have carried wrongly in your flesh or emotions. He is washing these burdens to the foot of his cross. And as He covers your arms He is giving you the strength to carry the burdens he gives you, but only in your spirit and only as far as His cross as He intended. As He flows over your hands, He is placing healing in your hands. Everything you set your hand to do will prosper because he has touched it first.

As he continues to flow down he is covering your legs, giving you the strength to stand in adversity. As he washes over your feet he is preparing you to walk in peace. Everywhere you set your foot is holy ground for He has stepped there first. And just as water pools around the base of the glass so too the Holy Spirit is spreading out from around you so that anyone who gets within three feet of you can't help but feel His presence.

People will no longer see the spirit that is in you. Rather they will see you in the Holy Spirit in Jesus holy name. Amen."

Chapter 13: Demerit Badges, Shame Blame & Guilt

"The Scripture says, No man who believes in Him [who adheres to, relies on, and trusts in Him] will [ever] be put to shame or be disappointed."—Rom 10:11 (AMP)

"Even as [in His love] He chose us [actually picked us out for Himself as His own] in Christ before the foundation of the world, that we should be holy (consecrated and set apart for Him) and blameless in His sight, even above reproach, before Him in love."
–Eph 1:4 (AMP)

*"He [Jesus] was betrayed and put to death because of our misdeeds and was raised to secure our justification (our acquittal), [making our account balance and absolving us from **all guilt** before God]."* –Rom 4:25 (AMP)

These three are some of the most crippling forces at work in the church today. I share with clients that they are wearing sashes similar to cub / girl scouts and on these sashes are the badges for the things they have done. We point to one and say, "Oh this one, yeah this is when I did that thing, it was bad. Oh but *this* one, this one was *really bad*!" We compare our failings and our shortcomings without even understanding the effects we are having on our own character and on Christ's ability to redeem us.

Shame, blame, and guilt are wonderful *if* they lead us to the cross. We must realize however that this is *NOT* their intention. These three under the covering of condemnation want to drive us as far away from God and the cross of Christ as possible. We are quick to cover up our sin rather than repent because shame tells us,

"What would people think?" Blame tries to play the whole thing off, "It's not your fault anyway it's their fault." and then guilt hits us with, "Besides you know you also did x, y, and z before this, do you really think you can get before God?"

We must own our actions before we can disown them. Once we take ownership of our sin and repent God is faithful and just to forgive. But it all starts with ownership which means we must admit our guilt. Instead of blaming, we must confess and repent (shameful as it may seem), and *then* we can receive our forgiveness and newness of life.

Even if we are able somehow to take our sins to the cross these three like to hang on just to throw our shortcomings back in our faces in an attempt to make us less effective in the Kingdom of God. Condemnation causes us to shrink back from what God would have us do. It prevents us from giving that word of prophesy or encouragement. It binds us and paralyzes us from acting when God gives us direction. When we hold on to the shame, blame, and guilt of sins we have repented of we are entertaining the spirit of condemnation.

"There is therefore now no condemnation to those who are in Christ Jesus, who do not walk according to the flesh, but according to the Spirit." –Rom 8:1 (NKJV)

Even though this scripture is clear we often allow ourselves to be influenced by this spirit. When I came through deliverance I fell for what I have since named the 'trick' prayer. Since then I have used this tool to share with clients exactly how God views condemnation. I was led and repeated, "Heavenly Father I repent for ever sin I've ever committed from my conception to this very moment. But to show you how serious these sins were, I'm going to hold on to a little of the shame, a little of the blame, and a little of the guilt, just to prove how much I love you."

After a brief pause my mentor then asked me if I meant the prayer I just prayed. "Absolutely!" I blurted out. He then asked if it sounded funny to me at all. I thought about it and was able to say in all honesty it didn't sound funny to me at all. It made perfect sense. I had been raised on guilt and condemnation why would it sound anything other than perfectly natural. Then he explained, "You see when we hold on to the shame the blame and the guilt we think we are somehow being noble. God looks at this quite differently. He would say to you, 'Why would you shove the crown of thorns on my sons head again? Why would you lay open his back again? Why would you drive the nails through his hands and feet again? Why would you say that my son's horrid death on the cross wasn't enough, not only to take your sin, but to take away the shame, blame and guilt that go along with them?'"

I was stunned. I couldn't even answer. Then he led me in another prayer. I prayed, "Lord your word says that your people parish for a lack of knowledge. Well now I have that knowledge. I lay every sin I've ever committed along with its shame, blame and guilt at the foot of your cross. I receive my forgiveness in Jesus holy name." I can't even tell you the difference. It was as if he removed my 'demerit badge sash' and placed upon me a new royal sash in its place.

"But with me it is a very small thing that I should be judged by you or by a human court. In fact, I do not even judge myself."—1Cor 4:3 (NKJV)

Appropriate Applications of Comfort

Comforting those who suffer loss such as death, divorce, lost relationships must go through a grieving process. Don't try to short-circuit the client's pain. Don't try to give them advice on what they need to do to get over it. Remember we do not give advice! We can help by listening and sharing their hurt. (1Chronicles 19:3)

Comfort those who suffer shame. Ask the Lord to remove the shame and restore honor. The Lord removes the shame and guilt associated with the incident. He does not take away the memory just the pain and condemnation. Guilt is good because it gets us to the cross. After the cross, guilt becomes condemnation.

- Offer the opportunity of a clear conscience through repentance and forgiveness. Job 6:10
- Pray for good sleep. Psalm127:2
- Offer your faith when others are down 1 Thessalonians 3:2,7 invite them to trust in your faith that God will not throw them away. You might also refer them to Romans 3:3 that even if we lose all of our faith, God is still faithful.
- Allow them to be angry with God.
- Humor can release tension, but do not tease them. This will do more harm than good. Proverbs 26:18-19
- Music can comfort a person under oppression 1Samuel 16:23. The exception to this rule would be playing happy music to someone in depression. Proverbs 25:20. Spiritual gifts such as prophecy help comfort the spirit. 1Corinthians 14:3,31
- Burden bearing to absorb and carry the burdens of the other is acceptable (but only as far as the cross). Galatians 6:2, 5
- Pray for justice. Forgiveness allows the Lord to be in charge, eliminates the clients' sense of vengeance and sets the client free.

We are to comfort those who lack hope. We are to speak kindly and encouragingly to all clients. Isaiah 40:1-2, Hosea 2:14. Present God's assurances from the word, not as clichés' but as the Lord prompts. Psalms

119:52, 76; Romans 15:4. Be a safe and caring person, reflecting Jesus. Be God's love "with skin on". Galatians 5:22-25

- Use the authority of Jesus Christ to hold clients accountable and to protect them. Psalm 23:4
- Give practical help. Be aware of church and community resources. James 1: 5; 2: 16-17.
- If your testimony is similar to the client's then share briefly to reassure them that there is hope.
- Comfort with the comfort with which you were comforted Acts 16:40; II Corinthians 1:4.
- Teach what is right Isaiah 57:18
- Pray, fighting for your client Colossians 2:2
- Be a father/mother in Christ, providing a safe place to grow. Parenting in Christ does not create childish dependency. I Thessalonians 5:11

There is great comfort in God's sovereign actions. Ultimately, it is He who heals and comforts. When a person is healed rejoice, but if a person is not as healed as you would like, trust that the Lord has not forgotten, and He always completes what He has started. God will pursue His child. Isaiah 49:13; Acts 9:31

Inappropriate Application of Comfort

We do not want to gang up on those who wounded the client. "Yes they should be horse whipped for doing those things to a child." You might say "yes you have a right to be angry, but if you give up that right, you will be set free" Forgiveness sets you free. It does not condone what happened to you, nor does it ask you to put yourself in a position to be hurt again. It simply says that I am giving up the right to be angry with someone who has hurt me.

- Attitudes or acts of vengeance. Genesis 27:42, Psa 73.
- We do not support positive confession or will power alone. Job9: 27 don't over compliment. It can set performance-oriented people up for further fleshly striving.
- Talking too much, and pat answers tend to irritate and can force pain into deeper hiding places. Job16:2
- Visualization or false words do harm to the client. We do not ask God to erase any memories or change the outcome of incidents in an attempt to make the client feel safe. Job 21:34, Zechariah 10:2
- Bad timing is trying to get the client to feel better or release pain too soon or too late Isaiah 22:4. This is not about feelings. It is about a sovereign act of Almighty God. It is not to make the PDM feel better, by seeing the client loosed from bad feelings.
- Comfort without repentance helps the client stay stuck. This is like love without truth. Isaiah 57:6-13.
- Some substitutes for God can be mindless or immoral pleasures, occultism, hypnosis, ESP, food, shopping, drugs or any other addiction.
- Sexual relationships with clients are not appropriate ever. Lamentations 1:2

Recommended Questions

- Is there anything you feel God has forgiven you for that you're having a hard time forgiving yourself for?
- Are there any traumatic incidents from childhood that still bother you?
- Is there anything we haven't talked about, understanding that if you leave it in the dark Satan can still use it against you, anything you bring into the light God is ready and willing to release you from?

(Shame Blame & Guilt come through many of the actions and judgments made in childhood, be listening for signs of their presence throughout the interview as well)

Sample Prayers

Have Client Repeat: "You say in Your Word Lord that if we repent, You are faithful and just to forgive. And I receive your forgiveness. But to show You how sincere I am and how serious these sins were, I'm going to hang on to a little bit of the shame, blame, guilt, and regret just to show You how much I love you."

Spoken over Client: "You may not have said these words, but you told me you could not forgive yourself or still had regret for past sins. When you do this, Satan falls over laughing and God sees this in a totally different way. God says, **client**, why would you pull my son's beard out of His face once again? ...jam the crown of thorns on His head once again? ... Lay His back open and drive the nails through His wrists and feet? Why would you say that My Son's horrid death on the cross for you wasn't good enough? Not just to wash away your sin, but also the shame, blame, guilt, and regret associated with those sins."

Have Client Repeat: "Lord, you say in Your Word (in Hosea 4:6) that My people are destroyed for a lack of knowledge. Well, now we have that knowledge. We lay every sin we have ever committed from the day of our birth to this very moment at the foot of your cross, along with its shame, blame, guilt, and regret.

Father, I ask forgiveness for every sin that I have ever committed." (Have the client confess all of the sins that they shared with you during the interview adultery, stealing lying, etc. If abortion was involved, make sure they pray, "Forgive me Lord for murdering my baby."

Chapter 14: Forgiving Christians.

"For now we see in a mirror, dimly, but then face to face. Now I know in part, but then I shall know just as I also am known." 1Cor 13:12 (NKJV)

"Not that anyone has seen the Father, except He who is from God; He has seen the Father." –John 6:46 (NKJV)

"I speak what I have seen with My Father, and you do what you have seen with your father."—John 8:38 (NKJV)

Our relationship with Father God is founded on our relationship with our natural father. If our father was seen as abusive, short tempered, harsh, vindictive, selfish, demanding, unappeasable and the like, then that is how we will see God. It is our parents, particularly fathers, who model who and what God is to their children. This is why we are given the commands

"Train up a child in the way he should go, And when he is old he will not depart from it."
--Prov 22:6 (NKJV)

"You shall teach them [commandments] diligently to your children, and shall talk of them when you sit in your house, when you walk by the way, when you lie down, and when you rise up."—Deut 6:7 (NKJV)

"And you, fathers, do not provoke your children to wrath, but bring them up in the training and admonition of the Lord." –Eph 6:4 (NKJV)

Fathers are responsible to teach children about God. How we as parents see God will greatly effect what we teach our children. As none of us has seen him we can only *rely* on what the Bible says about Him. We need know that God loves us but we need know that whom the Father loves he chastens. We must understand that He is our provision, but that he expects us to labor. We are sons and daughters but we have not inherited the Kingdom yet. He loves us unconditionally but loves us too much to leave us in our current state.

In our infancy and childhood, mothers and fathers model a picture of God for us. How our parents act and what they do is how we "see" what God is like. We interpret each succeeding experience through the lens of judgments we have made, and the expectations we have developed in response to the relationship that we have with our parents. When bitterness and judgments are lodged in our hearts, our perception of God becomes distorted and our relationship with Him becomes crippled. If our hearts are pure we will be able to comprehend the glorious nature of God and relate to Him in blessed intimacy.

If we have made many judgments, our views of life and God become distorted. By the time we reach adulthood our mind has been taught to believe that it is God's desire to love and bless us, however, our heart says, "OH, yeah? He's just like dad (or mom). We are not capable of seeing life the way it really is. We have colored lenses attached to our eyes. We see everything from a wounded or distorted view. The lenses can only be removed after there is confession, repentance, forgiveness and the habits; patterns and structures have been put to death on the cross. Once this is accomplished God will be seen clearly, because we will have received a new heart and mind.

Ideally the parent's role, and particularly fathers, is to build each child through love, care, nurture, encouragement, discipline, teaching, holding accountable, and drawing limits and boundaries. Unfortunately this isn't always the case, and even if you had a perfect father, a child's perception isn't always based in truth.

The image of an uncaring parent is projected upon God. When a client asks the following questions:
- Why would God allow this thing to happen to me?
- Where was God when this occurred?
- Why does God hate me?

Telling the client that, "God cannot over-ride anyone's will." And asking them, "He didn't over-ride your will when you decided to sin, did He?" starts the process of rethinking who God is in their life. Sharing with them that, "He was there and He kept you alive, because He knew that one-day you would choose to be set free." begins the healing process in the relationship between the client and God.

When parents heap blame and fear on a child as they are growing up children respond with "I'd better not make a mistake or else!" When the child becomes an adult, they have a bitter root expectation that God will treat them in the same manner. They cannot relax or be spontaneous with God. They become a protective, rebellious and fearful adult.

Forgiving Wounds in the Church

Unfortunately whole denominations have won converts by hellfire and damnation preaching, trying to "scare sinners straight." The problem with this is that God *IS* love. Those that are his need to walk in that love not only for God but for sinners as well. Jesus did not come to condemn the world but rather that the world might be saved through him. If you have fallen victim to this form of evangelism I am sorry.

The church has hurt countless people. 'Hurting people hurt people', 'Sheep Bite', and other such sayings have come to me from so many directions I can't even keep track of them all. The hurts caused by Christians and Church Leadership must be forgiven for healing to come.

The Spirit of Elitism

Another of the forces running rampant in the church today is a spirit of Elitism. This spirit born of pride looks down its nose at anything it did not conceive. Those under the influence of this spirit feel as though they know better than everyone else. They may feel as though they have had some special revelation and are generally un-teachable as a result. In the church this spirit divides by telling those under its influence, "If they only knew what *we* know." Or "Oh bless their hearts for trying but we do it so much better." Of course it may not manifest in such obvious ways. It can simply refuse ministry from someone, or speak in a condescending tone to others in similar ministries and callings. It puffs up and will put others in their place if given opportunity.

Whenever a group, ministry, or church believes they've been given some sort of special revelation or feel that they fill a special need in the body of Christ a spirit of Elitism is in operation. This prideful spirit comes to puff up and convinces leaders that others may have a place in ministry but it isn't as important as their own. It attempts to subjugate and minimize the ministry contributions of others.

These leaders, so deceived, become increasingly difficult to reach with words of correction. Any such attempts are met with resistance and accusations that the one with the corrective word is operating as "Jezebel" trying to control and manipulate them. Sadly it is the leader under the influence of the spirit of

Elitism who is controlling and manipulating those in their care. The leader under this spirits influence is like the shepherds being chastened in Ezekiel 34.

They are no longer shepherding so much as they are taking advantage of the sheep. This False Shepherding Spirit causes leaders to seek their own agenda / vision over tending the sheep. Even if the vision was God given or inspired it is never more important than the people in the leaders care. Tending the sheep is the first responsibility of the shepherd. This calling comes before building programs, ministry expansion, global outreach, or anything else that a leader may feel the Lord has called them to. A Godly leader is called to tend and build up the body of Christ.

"He who is faithful in a very little [thing] is faithful also in much, and he who is dishonest and unjust in a very little [thing] is dishonest and unjust also in much."
–Luke 16:10 (AMP)

Leaders are to nurture and encourage the gifts of the people in their care, equipping them for the work of the ministry. Leaders under the influence of demonic spirits try to ignore the fact that all are capable of hearing from God and discourage the people from trying.

Those who escape from this type of leadership need to address the possibility of a spirit of False Submission being active in their lives. Submission isn't doing exactly what you're told, when you're told, and how you're told. It is being open to others so that God may speak to you through whomever He chooses.

Often when these spirits are at work they bring with them several others including: False Covering, False Yoke, False Responsibility, Control, Witchcraft, False Brotherhood, Fear, Fear of Rejection, Grief, Abortion (If not allowed to operate in spiritual gifts), Guilt, Shame, Condemnation, False Martyr Spirit (suffering wrongdoing for Jesus), Deception, Deaf and Dumb Spirit.

Can all these spirits really be at work in a believer's life? Absolutely! Remember the enemy wants nothing short of your destruction. When the door is opened to the enemy he is going to come and in force. Remembering that every client is different and that this is a partial list of possible forces aligning themselves against the client it is important to allow the Holy Spirit lead us in casting these and any others that are afflicting the client.

None of us has the whole counsel of God. *For now we know in part.* The Lord showed me a vision once of the denominations in the Body of Christ as different organs. Eyes, hands, feet, ears, etc. What he showed me was that denominations had essentially stemmed from differing parts of the body refusing to understand and except others. Consequently we have all of the eyes in this church, all of the hands in another, etc. It isn't that either is entirely right or wrong. Rather each encounters God and the world around them differently. Hands are not for seeing and eyes are not for clapping, each has a distinct purpose and use. That doesn't mean they will be comfortable worshiping together. He then went on to show me that I was but a cell in that part of the body he has placed me. Often when we get in trouble with the spirit of Elitism it is because we become deluded into thinking we are the whole hand rather than a cell in the hand.

Have you ever noticed how much more God moves in services, revivals, etc. where the body of Christ comes together across denominational lines? It is because the Body is coming together and each part fitly joined is greater than any one part separately.

Identifications of Love

Identifications of love are those words, gestures, actions and attitudes we interpret as love from others. These "packages" are idols, which define and limit our idea of what true love is; they almost assuredly deny us the full joy of giving and receiving it. When we demand these "packages" of love from those around us, we practice unregenerate love.

Father God created us to receive love. When love comes as He designed it, we can identify it properly for what it actually is. We do this through affection, wise discipline, and affirmation; and we will see sacrificial love demonstrated. When we don't receive proper love, we identify it as whatever we get from the primary people in our lives. We might see love as abuse, criticism, battering, and neglect. This then becomes our substitutes for love, and attention.

Every identification of love that is not God designed sacrificial love can be harmful.

Identifications of love in marriage

Who we are in Christ is largely determined by how we receive love. False identifications of love give us a false sense of who we are to God. Many are familiar with the 'Five Love Languages' made popular by Gary Chapman. These languages stem from our childhoods, and how we were shown love by our parents and consequently how we expect to receive it from others.

Words of Affirmation

Those whose 'love language' is 'words of affirmation' in many cases had one or more parent(s) who were critical. The opposite can also be true in some instances, that a parent was doting. In most cases however the child felt unable to please mom or dad and consequently cherishes words of affirmation above all else. Scriptures that assure the client of who they are in Christ will be very helpful in redefining this view of love.

Quality Time

The client was not made a priority. The parents may have needed alone time when they got home from work or had chores around the house to do before spending time with the child. Parents may have spent time with the child but only doing things the parent wanted / needed to do. Spending time making the client feel like they are a priority, being on time for appointments, and going out of your way to make time for a client will help the client feel like a priority to you. Having the client spend time in the word, prayer and worship with the Lord will bring the most healing.

Receiving Gifts

These clients had very little growing up or had parents that only showed love by giving presents. Selfishness and greed are the roots at work here. When money is tight or gifts aren't lavished upon them they don't feel loved. God has given gifts, financial, emotional, spiritual, and even his own son that we might be saved. Bringing the client to the understanding that it is better to give than to receive is essential.

Acts of Service

One of the most difficult groups to minister to are those whose love language is 'acts of service' because as Christians we are taught to be servants. We are taught that *"If anyone desires to be first, he shall be last of all and servant of all."(Mark 9:35, NKJV)* This is true, but it is not the service that is the problem. The problem lies in the motive behind the service. If we are serving to receive acceptance, affection or attention, we are serving with wrong heart motives. When we serve we are to serve as unto the Lord without expectation of reciprocation, reward, or anything in return. When we receive love in this form we are requiring the other to perform for our affection. In either case a structure of performance orientation is usually present. One or both parents may have required the child to perform for affection. The Judgment once made then creates the expectation that love equals works.

Physical Touch

The root of this language is found in either an absence / deficiency of physical touch or in inappropriate touch as a child. In the first case the child was starved for physical affection, cuddling, hugging, holding, carrying etc. These completely normal and needed forms of affection help to engage the child's emotions in a healthy manner. The child's spirit engages life in these actions. In the second case the child was violated and their sexuality awakened well before the time. In this case sexual promiscuity, homosexuality, and other perversions can result. The child grows up equating love with a physical relationship but may have great difficulty engaging emotionally, or spiritually. They may view themselves or others as objects for physical gratification. The opposite extreme of this may also be true. The client has great difficulty engaging in *any* physicality in the relationship fearing physical touch all together (though in this case the love language is *not* going to be 'physical touch').

Gender and identification of love

A man often identifies love by what his mother did. He may unconsciously demand that his wife fulfill that picture. He may have formed an identification of love based on fantasy. Sometimes a boy needs to believe that his mother was much more noble, holy, righteous, loving or comforting than she actually was. Thus he may make demands based on a picture of love formed out of that fantasy, as opposed to what was truly received.

A woman often identifies love by what her father did or did not do, and measures her husband's love by that standard.

The dynamic of counter balance

A dynamic in all relationships, especially in marriage is similar to a seesaw. For example one partner may be very talkative, and the other is silent; because of the silence the talkative partner talks even more. When away from the partner the silent one talks freely and vice versa. Together, neither is free to be themselves.

One may be a strict disciplinarian, so the other withholds, or placates and mediates. This causes the first to discipline more; and so on… One may become super religious; the other counters by becoming more earthly and worldly. This causes the first to be more "spiritual," and so on….. Here is the game people play: If only two are playing one is the *victim* and the other the *victimizer*, and in the course of the argument you might change roles. If three are playing we add *vindicator*. Dad comes home from work hearing his son speaking disrespectfully to his mother, (the son is the victimizer, the mother being the victim) dad becomes vindicator (avenger/protector) chastising his son for being disrespectful, the son now becomes the victim of dad's wrath who has just become the victimizer, and now mom becomes the vindicator who tells dad that he is just too hard on the boy, turning dad into the victim, and now mom is the victimizer, and the son feels sorry for the dad and he becomes the vindicator defending dad's actions. In the above example if Dad had come in and mediated the situation rather than vindicating mom the whole situation would have dissipated. Dad calmly sitting both the son and mom down to get the whole story, can then address both the sons disrespect and the situation that caused it without role reversal taking place.

Putting Our Identification of Love to Death on the Cross may not change the way that we do things, or the way we are, but it can transform the way we react to our spouse. There won't be that bitter root expectation that my spouse will never meet my need. There will be a greater ability to receive the love that your spouse shows as their expression of love. We will be able to ask for what we need and it will be enough, because that wrong identification will have been put to death on the cross.

Until unregenerate love dies

- We can't be free to be ourselves with each other
- We feel imprisoned, controlled, measured and judged.
- We unconsciously counterbalance each other and thus are never really in balance.
- We live in a world of tension, frequently trying to anticipate demands and potential criticisms.
- We cannot be real, having to "act out" whatever may please or placate the other.
- We will manipulate, push and pull; trying to force the other to fulfill what we think will make us feel loved.

Unregenerate love is:

- Use - manipulation, exploitation, demand, control and possession
- Idolatry - we worship a "form" of love rather than leaving ourselves open to the true love of God. We try to enslave others to the worship of those same idols.
- A source of fire to heat the furnace of our anger when others refuse to give in.
- Selfish rather than sacrificial is unregenerate love. Unregenerate love makes demands. Sacrificial love lays down life for others.

Identifications of love are formed out of snapshots from childhood. When the expressions of love we've experienced are profuse and varied, we learn to recognize and receive love in many packages. It is when love has been handed out sparingly that we latch on to a few meager expressions and turn them into idols.

Sharing identifications of love can be a fine way for a husband and wife to learn to know one another; it can create closeness and understanding, and can truly be fun. The "Love Languages" Touch, Acts of Service, Gifts, Quality Time, Words of Affirmation constitute "unregenerate love" Because they are not sacrificial, they are those things that we need in order to feel loved. Even though they appear to be wholesome identifications of love, it is crucial to remember that all human love must be redeemed on the cross. In prayer, mates can come to see the idols they have tried to force upon one another. They will recognize how they have defiled one another, and can then repent and ask forgiveness.

Forgiving Christians

"For if you forgive men their trespasses, your heavenly Father will also forgive you. But if you do not forgive men their trespasses, neither will your Father forgive your trespasses." –Matt 6:14-15 NKJV

"Lord, how often shall my brother sin against me, and I forgive him? Up to seven times?" Jesus said to him, "I do not say to you, up to seven times, but up to seventy times seven." Matt 18:21-22 NKJV

"And his master was angry, and delivered him to the torturers until he should pay all that was due to him. "So My heavenly Father also will do to you if each of you, from his heart, does not forgive his brother his trespasses."—Matt 18:34-35 NKJV

It is hard enough to deal with the hurts and wounds caused by unbelieving people. Harder still is forgiving those who we deem should know better. We've all been hurt in church at some time or another. The truth is wounded people wound people. Many of the people that come to us for prayer have been mistreated and often rejected in the church, either by leaders or other Christians.

"…Now I know in part (imperfectly), but then I shall know and understand fully and clearly, even in the same manner as I have been fully and clearly known and understood [by God]." –1Cor 13:12

It is imperative to forgive to be forgiven and with that in mind it is necessary to forgive any Christians, pastors, elders, deacons, etc. who may have given us misinformation about who and what God is. We all know in part according to the scripture and we are all fallible. Consequently we may share what we believe to be the truth with others only to have that truth exposed later as falsehood. This is why leaders are held to a higher accountability in scripture. Leaders are in the position to do great good and great harm to the body of Christ. Leaders need to be constantly before the Lord and in His Word to ensure they have the most accurate image of Him as possible so they can present Christ in balance. Even the best leaders however sometimes get it wrong. It is then that they require correction, and forgiveness.

Once we are able to forgive those who have given us a faulty picture of who God is then it is necessary to ask the Lord to reveal himself to us. To show us who he really is and what he is really about. As the client forgives and repents for their faulty beliefs it falls on the prayer minister to declare God's identity to the client.

Recommended Questions:

- How old were you when you accepted the Lord?
- If you died today, where would you be?
- If Jesus stood at the gate, and asked "Why should I let you into my Heaven?" What would your answer be?
- If you read the Word a little more, would God be more pleased with you?
- Have you ever disappointed God?
- Have you ever been mad at God?
- Have you ever been involved in a church split?
- Do you know what your love language is?
- Were you ever touched inappropriately as a child?
- When did you first have sex? Was it consensual? With someone your own age?
- Did you become promiscuous when you got older?
- Have you ever left a church angry?
- Has anyone called into question your salvation?

Sample Prayers:

Have Client Repeat: "Heavenly Father I confess I have no idea who you are. I have judged you and have believed the lies taught to me by others who said they knew you. Lord I repent for my judgments and I put the lies to death on your cross. I ask you to forgive me and to reveal yourself to me in a whole new way."

Spoken over Client: "As you have confessed and repented, I speak the forgiveness of Almighty God over you. The Lord is erasing every lie you have believed about him. He is replacing these lies with his truth. That he is a father who will never leave you nor forsake you. He is your defender and protector. He is a perfectly safe place to lie down and rest. He is your provider. He loves you not because of anything you have done but because he created you and he can't help himself."

Have Client Repeat: "Father I confess I don't know how to love. My identifications of love are **(specifics from interview i.e. sex, sacrificing self, degrading self, being used, neglected, hurt, abused, rejected, mate being unavailable, controlled by mate, and being manipulated).** I repent and ask you Lord to redefine love for and in me. Help me Lord to love as you do, sacrificially and unconditionally."

Have Client Repeat: "I forgive all Christians who hurt me, and all the hypocrisy that I have seen in Christianity and ministry, including my parents, pastors, deacons, elders, etc. I forgive every Christian who has fed me misinformation concerning who and what God is, and I put to death on the cross my identification of who and what God is, as well my identification of what love is."

Spoken over Client: "The Lord is washing away your old identifications of love and renewing your heart to receive the love of Almighty God, pure, holy, righteous, and unconditional love. Now the Lord is taking you to the resurrection side of the cross and you are seeing Father God in a whole new way. You see Him as a Father, who will never leave you nor forsake you, reject you, defile you, abandon you, or harm you. You see Him as a Father who will always be there for you, always love you, nurture you, and hear you. He has made you a number one priority in His life. Since He has made you a priority, you can be a priority, and if someone tries to make you a priority, you can allow them to. You are good enough, smart enough, worthy enough, and worthwhile enough. Not because of who you are, but because of whose you are.

You are standing before Almighty God as an empty vessel, because you put to death on His cross, your identification of whom and what He is, as well as what your identification of what love is."

Have Client Repeat: "Father, send your Holy Spirit to fill this empty vessel. Fill me with the wisdom, truth, knowledge, and character of Almighty God. I want to experience Your compassion, mercy, and grace. Now fill this empty vessel with the love of Almighty God ... pure, holy, and righteous love. Lord make me whole, so that I don't need anyone to fill an empty place in me. I put to death on your cross my need to be needed. Fill me with Your love to such overflowing that I can allow my (future) husband/wife to be free to be themselves. He/she no longer has to perform to fulfill my desires or be what I need him/her to be, but rather he/she can give what he/she has, and I can receive it. I am whole and I am free to be myself, not what everyone expects me to be."

Chapter 15: Soul Ties & Sexual Sins

"When David had finished speaking to Saul, the soul of Jonathan was knit with the soul of David, and Jonathan loved him as his own life." –1Sam 18:1 (AMP)

Soul ties are the bonds that join us spiritually in relationship. They are formed through shared traumatic, intimate, or deeply personal experiences. When we form these ties we in effect give the other person a piece of our spirit and take within us a piece of theirs. A bond is formed like an invisible chord or bridge connecting us in the spirit. Soul ties can be formed in three areas: spiritually, emotionally and physically, and in these three areas they can be Godly or ungodly. A Godly soul tie will draw us closer to God and His plan for our lives. An ungodly soul tie will draw us towards fulfilling our fleshly desires and thereby pulling us further from a deep relationship with God. Picture soul ties as a net. Godly soul ties form beneath us keeping us from falling and lifting us higher. Ungodly soul ties form a net above us keeping us from the heights the Lord would have us attain. In many cases this drags us down from heights we have already achieved.

Physical

Soul Ties that affect us physically are the most common of the three. God created sex for a man and woman to become one in marriage. *"Therefore a man shall leave his father and his mother and shall become united and cleave to his wife, and they shall become one flesh. (Gen 2:24,* AMP*).* A physical soul tie is formed through physical intimacy with another. There is only one Godly form of this soul tie and that is in marriage. All others are ungodly and need to be repented of and severed.

When we ask clients how many people they have had sex with it is not to embarrass them. We are trying to determine how fractured their soul may be and how many soul ties in this area need to be broken. Having the client name the individual aloud (first names only) allows us to lead them in confession and to sever these soul ties specifically. Homosexuality and other sexual perversions have other more complicated issues involved and will be addressed later in this chapter.

Emotional

Emotional soul ties are formed in romantic relationships and deep friendships. Sharing the most intimate details of ourselves and our lives with others takes trust and commitment in a relationship. A soul tie is formed when the relationship reaches this level. Tied friends for example, 'know' what the other is feeling even if no words are shared and the other is trying to mask their true feelings. Emotional soul ties are not as easy to identify as physical and while they often accompany physical soul ties, they can be formed independent of them. An example of a Godly emotional soul tie would be that of a spiritual mom /dad, a man or woman who takes the client under their wing so to speak to love them and raise them up in the things of God. Ungodly emotional soul ties can be formed with unsaved friends or through unhealthy romantic relationships. Anyone with whom we share our most intimate feelings, dreams, and aspirations we have likely formed a soul tie with.

Ungodly soul ties need to be severed and the relationships limited if not ended all together. When severing ungodly soul ties it is necessary to send back to the other person what is theirs and to call back the pieces of the client's soul they have taken. Better to sever an earthly relationship entirely than to let it sever your relationship with God. Understandably we cannot cut off unsaved family but they should not be allowed to undo influence in our relationships with God or others.

When one is married and has an emotional soul tie with a member of the opposite sex, it can easily turn into emotional adultery. Adultery is not confined to the physical relationship. When a married spouse shares their deep feelings, dreams and needs with a friend of the opposite sex instead of their spouse an emotional soul tie will form. Any relationship that threatens the marriage needs to be ended. Does this mean we can't have friends outside of marriage? No, it means that our spouse is the one we are to connect with to have our emotional needs met.

Spiritual

These soul ties are formed frequently through religious affiliations, church, the occult, etc. Spiritual ties are often formed between intercessors and those they intercede for on a regular basis. They can be formed between ministers and the people they minister to. Prayer partners, small groups, and even whole churches can form spiritual soul ties.

When we give someone spiritual authority to speak into our lives we make ourselves vulnerable to them and thus form a tie to them. This should be life giving, but it can end in disaster. A godly soul tie will bring us higher into the things of God, but if a religious spirit, a spirit of elitism or other unclean spirits are operating thru the authority it can be very detrimental. Once we recognize these false spirits we are tied to they will need to be severed. The client needs to repent for false submission and whoever the client was spiritually tied to needs to be forgiven.

Homosexuality & Other sexual perversion

Regardless of social, political, or religious leanings the Bible calls homosexuality sin; more than that it calls it an abomination. I will not get into the debate of whether someone is born a homosexual or whether they 'choose' it as a lifestyle. Such arguments are fruitless and irrelevant. The fact remains that it is a sinful lifestyle with terrible ramifications not the least of which as a fragmented spirit through soul ties. Let's lay to rest the argument by addressing the roots of both sides.

I was born this way

"The ungodly are perverse and estranged from the womb; they go astray as soon as they are born, speaking lies."—Psa 58:2-4 AMP

I never argue with anyone who says they were 'born this way' I simply agree that in all likelihood they were. I then proceed to explain to them how judgments in the womb can cause a child to adopt gender qualities, mannerisms, etc of those desired by the parent. If mom really wants a girl and the child is a boy they may act effeminate. Conversely a girl may be very tom-boyish.

Spiritual rebellion and the structure of performance orientation play a huge role in these clients. The judgment that "You made me wrong God." or "I won't be loved if I'm not (the opposite of what God made them)" begins the cycle that will ultimately lead them into the homosexual lifestyle.

They chose that lifestyle

In my experience it is rare for people to choose homosexuality without some form of wound, incident, or exposure to the demonic influence behind it. Clients who were sexually abused or molested may be very susceptible to the principality of homosexuality. A young person experimenting with their own sexuality who engages in a homosexual act opens a door for the enemy to come. In a society with increasingly weakening morals it is not uncommon for young people to experiment with sex in a variety of ways. Once the door has been opened to sexual immorality, sexual perversion, or homosexuality those spirits *are* going to come in and even if the person was 'only experimenting' they may find themselves unable to escape the urges and desires these unclean spirits stir up in their physical bodies. Homosexuality and other sexual perversion results, taking more and more ground in the persons life with each relationship. The person may even say 'they chose' this lifestyle but it was the demonic influences which in fact chose them and are keeping them captive.

As with all other sinful practices however there is forgiveness and restoration at the cross. If someone comes to you seeking help in this area, cast the spirits at work into the pit where they belong and lead the client in prayers of confession, repentance and forgiveness.

Recommended Questions:

- How old were you when you became sexually active?
- Was it consensual? With someone your own age?
- Did you become promiscuous?
- How many sexual partners have you had? (Ask for first names)
- Were you touched inappropriately as a child?
- Do you have any friends who you feel are closer than a brother / sister?
- Have you ever been hurt in the church?
- Have you ever been hurt / betrayed by a friend?
- Do you have any strong relationships with unbelievers?
- Have you been involved in the occult?
- Are you part of a ministry in the church?
- Do you operate in any spiritual gifts?

Sample Prayers:

Have Client Repeat: "Father you created sex for a husband and wife. I confess that I used it for my own satisfaction and pleasure. I repent Lord for using it wrongly. In doing so Lord I formed soul ties with (List names from interview). Father I ask you to sever every ungodly soul tie I have made. I freely give back what is theirs and I ask you Lord to take back what is mine. Restore me Lord and make me whole that I may give myself to my husband / wife (Or future husband / wife if not married)."

Spoken over Client: "The Lord is taking his severe sword and he is severing every ungodly soul tie you have formed with these men / women. He is sending back to them what is theirs' voiding every claim they hold on you and shutting every door they have used to gain access to you. What he shuts no one may open."

Have Client Repeat: "Father I repent for my ungodly relationships. These relationships have been unhealthy and have drawn me away from you. Father I allowed my relationships to become idols that I placed before you and I humbly repent. Father, sever every ungodly soul tie I have formed with (Specifics from interview). I freely give back to them what is theirs and I ask you to restore to me that which is mine in Jesus holy name."

Spoken over Client: "As you have repented for your idolatrous relationships the Lord is taking his severe sword and smashing these idols. He is severing every ungodly soul tie you have formed with (specifics from interview). The Lord is sending back to them what is theirs, cancelling every spiritual assignment, debt and claim that they hold over you.

Now Heavenly Father as (client) has freely sent back what is theirs I call to the north, south, east and west and I call (client's) spirit back in Jesus holy name. The Lord is knitting your mind together with your soul and your spirit and he is making you whole, complete, and able to give yourself completely to your husband / wife ("the one God has for you" if not married)."

Have Client Repeat: "Heavenly Father I repent for my involvement in (sexual perversions). As an act of my will and by the authority of Jesus Christ I cast far from me (specifics from interview i.e. the Homosexual spirit, Sexual Perverse Spirits, Incubus, Succubus, etc) never to return. I ask you Lord now to cleanse my mind body soul and spirit from all defilement. Father, send your Holy Spirit to fill me to overflowing with your love, mercy, grace, kindness, forgiveness, life and light in Jesus holy name."

Spoken over Client: "As you have repented the Lord is faithful and just to forgive. I speak the forgiveness of Almighty God over you. The Lord is driving these spirits from you never to return. He is loosing His key of David shutting every door the enemy has used to gain entrance into you and what he shuts no one may open. The Lord is renewing your mind and reforming your identity in Him. He is speaking assurance to your spirit that he did not form you wrong and that you *are exactly* who he has called you to be. He is removing all ungodly impulses and desires restoring you to the perfect plan he had for you from the foundation of the world.

Chapter 16: Standing in Repentance

Just as Daniel repented for all of his ancestors and his nation in Daniel chapter nine, so it falls to us as ministers of healing to stand in for all Christians, the client's parents, and any others whom the client has ought against, repenting and asking their forgiveness. This may very well be the most powerful aspect of the ministry session.

Daniel prayed, "We have sinned" and when he prayed the angel of the Lord came to him. In the years I have been ministering in this way I have never seen him not show up in the session at this time. Beginning with all Christians, then moving to mom, then dad, and finally racially, we repent for whatever judgments the client has shared with us.

Christians

We stand in for any Christians, leaders, pastors, elders, ministers, etc. who ever hurt the client. We repent for giving them faulty information about who God is, for misusing, mistreating, abusing, or in any other way harming them. We then ask the client to forgive us. When they do we speak the forgiveness of Almighty God over them; as they have forgiven so to now they can be forgiven according to Matthew chapter six.

Mom & Dad

Wounds from mom and dad go deep. It isn't enough to have the client repent for the judgments they made. Repenting allows the Lord to reap what we have sown but healing comes form hearing those judgments back in the form of confession. When we stand in repentance we are giving the client the opportunity to confront the person that caused them such pain.

I was ministering recently in Lakeland Florida at the outpouring there. I was praying for David, a man easily ten years my senior. When he shared with me some of the trauma he suffered at the hands of his mother I was rocked to my core. I could scarcely believe how bad his childhood had been. I led him in prayers of confession and repentance of the judgments he made and in prayers of forgiveness for his mother and I saw no visible change in his countenance. The Lord then told me to stand in for his mother and to confess and repent on her behalf. It was certainly unexpected given that we were in altar ministry but I obeyed. I told David that I was going to stand in as a spiritual mother (which got a look of genuine confusion) and I began to confess and repent for all of the sins he had just shared with me. He began to cry uncontrollably. When I asked him if he could forgive me he nearly collapsed in my arms. "I forgive you mom." He sobbed. I then proceeded to speak a mothers blessing over him and when we stopped holding each other I could see the visible change in his countenance. He was set free.

By standing in we put flesh on the judgments the client has made. We give voice to things that probably are unspoken but not forgotten. We allow them the opportunity to forgive face to face those that they may not be able to otherwise.

When Melissa and I minister together I have her stand in as spiritual mom and I as spiritual dad. While it saves a lot of funny looks it also serves the more practical purpose of credibility. A mother's blessing comes more genuinely from a woman and a fathers blessing is more convincing from a man.

Jesus sent his disciples out in two's and it is a good practice to minister in this fashion. This is not to say I haven't ministered alone. In fact I often do when ministering to another man but this has more to do with scheduling than anything else. There is power in receiving from both a male and female in the session. Ministers then become spiritual mom and dad restoring relationship and bringing freedom in a dynamic and powerful way. When possible I recommend ministering as a couple when married for this reason. For those who are unmarried and wish to partner in ministry with someone of the opposite gender my only caution is to be aware of the intimate and personal nature of this ministry. Do not let the anointing be confused with romantic feelings and be very aware of your own emotions. Spiritual soul ties can very easily be formed in this form of ministry and can quickly be confused for romantic feelings. This is not to discourage the practice only to advise so that you can be mindful and watchful.

Ethnicity

One of the most profoundly effective prayers I pray with people is forgiveness of those who have hurt them because of prejudice. God made all of us and no one race has anything over another. There is no room for bigotry in the Kingdom of God. I don't understand it nor tolerate it in my presence. When ministering to all of our clients but especially other ethnic groups it is important to ask what nationality / heritage they come from. We are looking for any signs of embarrassment or fear of rejection. In the course of praying we stand in repentance for everyone who has mistreated, abused, put down or in any other way made the client feel less of a person because of their heritage.

Recommended Questions:

- What kind of personalities did your brothers/sisters have i.e., angry, controlling, fearful, victims etc.
- Are your brothers and sisters married? If so, married more than once? (If yes) What broke up the first marriage? Other marriages... How is their current marriage? Are they happy? (Ask these questions for each sibling)
- Have you been married more than once? If so, what broke it up?
- If you could change one thing about your spouse, what would it be? What's the one thing your spouse would change about you?
- How do you get along with your children?
- Do you know what kind of pregnancy your mother had with you? Were you early, late, or any complications?
- What kind of work did your dad do while you were growing up?
- What kind of personality did your dad have? How about your mom?
- Were they ever abusive?
- Would mom and dad fight a lot? What would they fight about? Tell me how old you were, and then tell me what happened, and how you reacted.
- Growing up, did you feel as though you couldn't please your mom/dad?
- Who did the discipline?
- How would they handle it... with a switch, belt, or anything they could get their hands on?
- Did they ever lose control? Any unjust spankings?
- Would the other parent ever spank? How would they discipline?
- Did you ever end up taking care of your baby sister/brother? Did you resent it? How old were you?
- Any difficult or traumatic incidents in your childhood that trouble you now?
- Have you had any affairs? With a married person?
- Do you struggle with procrastination (putting off to the last minute those things that need to be done)?
- Did you have a problem with stealing, or lying as a child, or even as an adult?

Sample Prayers:

Spoken over Client: "(Client) I come to you now and I repent for every Christian, leader, pastor, elder, deacon (specifics from interview), who hurt you in His name. I repent for giving you false information about who he is and what it is to be a Christian. I repent for not allowing you to grow in and use you gifts in the church (and for any others that the interview or Holy Spirit reveal) can you forgive me?

(After the client forgives) As you have forgiven I now speak the forgiveness of Almighty God over you. The Lord is revealing himself to you and to your spirit filling you with His holy presence in Jesus holy name.

Spoken over Client: "Now (client) I come as your spiritual mom and I confess I (specifics from interview) can you forgive me?" (If client says "I forgive you mom" skip 'have client repeat' below)

Have Client Repeat: (Ask "Can you say,) "I forgive you mom?"

(After client forgives mom say) "Now I speak a mothers blessing over you (client). I say that you…

Spoken over Client: "Now I come to you as your spiritual dad and I confess I (specifics from interview) can you forgive me? (If client says "I forgive you dad" skip 'have client repeat' below)

Have Client Repeat: (Ask "Can you say,) "I forgive you dad?"

(After client forgives dad say) "Now I speak a fathers blessing over you (client). I call your spirit to life and you into the fullness of your manhood / womanhood. I call forth and bestow upon you your birthright. I say that you are the head and not the tail, above only and not beneath. You are blessed in the city and in the country, in the basket and in the store. Blessed is the fruit of your body. Your enemies come before you one way they will flee before you seven. The Lord prepares a table before you in the presence of your enemies. He anoints your head with oil and your cup runs over. You are smart enough, holy enough, lovable enough, and strong enough. You are accepted in the beloved. And any man / woman would be crazy not to want you on their arm. You are a son / daughter of the Most High God and I dedicate you to Him and His purposes this day. I say grow and be and do all that He has called you to be from the foundation of the World in Jesus holy name.

Spoken over Client: (If client showed any embarrassment about their nationality of origin) "I come to you and I repent for everyone who has put you down, made you feel inferior, or tried to put you in your place because of your race. God is no respecter of persons; he created all of us and loves all of us unconditionally and equally. Can you forgive me for my ignorance and cruelty?"

(After client forgives say) "Now (client) as you have forgiven so you too can be forgiven. I speak the forgiveness of almighty God over you I declare the blessings of almighty God over you, every physical, financial, emotional, and spiritual blessing over you and your household in Jesus holy name.

Chapter 17: Homework & Follow-up

"He cried aloud [with might] and said, Cut down the tree and cut off its branches; shake off its leaves and scatter its fruit. Let the living creatures flee from under it and the fowls from its branches."—Dan 4:14 AMP

Old habits don't just die they are replaced. Just as rotten trees in an orchard aren't just hewn down a new tree is planted in its place…

"For he shall be like a tree planted by the waters that spreads out its roots by the river; and it shall not see and fear when heat comes; but its leaf shall be green. It shall not be anxious and full of care in the year of drought, nor shall it cease yielding fruit."
—Jer 17:8 AMP

"…that they may be called oaks of righteousness [lofty, strong, and magnificent, distinguished for uprightness, justice, and right standing with God], the planting of the Lord, that He may be glorified." –Isa 61:3 AMP

When we have finished ministering to the client the ministry isn't finished. In fact, it has just begun. We have hewn down the old tree with its fruit and have planted a new tree. This new tree requires cultivation to grow lest it too yield fruit like its' predecessor. To this end we give every client that sits with us homework.

The homework is designed to continue the healing process. For 31 days the client is to faithfully and diligently commit to declarations of faith, prayers to cancel old structures and to establish new ones. Why 31 days? Popular psychology says it takes 21 days to form a habit. We give the client grace to take a week or so to get used to doing the work before actually doing it.

The homework consists of five parts:

Taking thoughts captive.

Whenever a negative thought comes into the clients mind we have them declare out loud, "Thank you Lord for taking care of that!" Clients are doing three things when they say this. Firstly they are trusting, "Lord, for the first time I am trusting that YOU will fight all of my battles." Secondly, they submit, "For the first time I take the fight out of me and lay it at the foot of the cross." Thirdly they rest, "For the first time in my life Lord, I am resisting the devil. I am not rebuking him, renouncing him, or casting him away. I am simply letting you deal with him on my behalf. Thank you Lord for taking care of that."

Watching words

"Death and life are in the power of the tongue, and they who indulge in it shall eat the fruit of it [for death or life]." –Prov 18:21 AMP

Because we have the power to speak life and death it is critical that we guard our speech. Whenever a negative word comes out of the client's mouth they are encouraged to say out loud, "CANCEL, I used to think that way, I used to feel that way, and I used to be that way, but not anymore, Thank you Lord for taking care of that." This simple statement owns where we came from in making the statement and yet gives God the grace to 'catch' the seed even before it hits the ground, preventing the harvest that would surely follow.

Positive affirmations

Each night before bed and each morning when the client gets up we encourage them to say out loud, "I CHOOSE THIS DAY TO TRUST IN GOD! I choose life! I choose life! I choose life! I choose blessings! I choose blessings! I choose blessings! I bind myself to God's love, peace, joy, glory, wisdom, hope, favor, strength, courage, and prosperity. I choose to walk in God's calling, anointing, plan and provision for my life in Jesus holy name.

Rightly Handling Emotions

It is important to remember that emotions and feelings are part of the autonomic nervous system, like blinking and breathing. We cannot control them, only direct them. We don't want to stuff our feelings because they will find a way to the surface sooner or later, usually in a self-destructive manner. There are NO unexpressed emotions. The best thing to do is: Own them, to disown them. Saying, "Lord, I take these emotions and feelings, (name them i.e., fear, rage, shame, blame, guilt, lust, unforgiveness, low self-esteem, etc) and I put them to death on your cross. Now come Holy Spirit and give me a glorious opposite. In my weakness is your strength"

These emotions and feelings are habits, patterns and structures. They are our Egypt. The Israelites cried so desperately to be free, and after only three (3) days they wanted to go back to Egypt. Why, because Egypt was so wonderful? NO. It was familiar. Sometimes, because of fear of the new walk, we will take familiar over freedom, even if the familiar was bad.

When we take in bitterness, anger, hurt, and unforgiveness, it is like you drinking poison waiting for some one else to die.

If someone has caused us hurt, anger, or offense, we absolutely have a right to these emotions, and feelings. And we MUST say ouch. Sharing with that person or if that is impossible then with someone, that they offended and or hurt our feelings. This sets us free from allowing the offense to be stuffed and fester, but if we entertain the above offense, pride can and will sneak in the back door. God can do nothing, but push down the proud. A humble person is not easily offended. We humble ourselves by putting anger, hurt, and offense to death on the cross. When we give up our right to these, God will exalt us, and even prepare a table before us in the presence of your enemies. It is better to be exalted by God than honored by man.

Keeping what was gained

The enemy tries to convince clients that this kind of freedom isn't real, that nothing has changed and that everything is the way it was. We have to understand that Satan is the accuser of the brethren. It's his job to throw our failings, shortcomings, and sins in our face. He does this to drive us away from Father God. Don't let him. When the enemy starts dredging up the past, starts giving you all the reasons you "can't get before God" let him. Then take all of those accusations, turn to your Heavenly Father and admit them; Confessing, repenting and receiving your forgiveness.

THANK YOU LORD FOR TAKING CARE OF THAT!

The Follow-up session

We encourage every client to follow up with us in two weeks. At that time we ask them to share with us one good thing that has occurred since their session, one bad thing and one *ugly* thing. We want the client to recognize the good that was accomplished before looking at what still needs work. And we want to finish with the area in which the client feels they have totally blown it. Many times we can pray with the client over the phone from this point. Sometimes another session is scheduled to bring the client back in. This is especially the case if the Lord has been working overtime to show the client other areas that they hadn't revealed in the first session. The format for a follow-up session is very free form and much more specific to the fruit being brought forth. This typically means this session and any subsequent ones are much shorter in duration. The fruit-to-root principle is applied as it would be in altar ministry to trace the specific problems to their source and deal with said source.

Bibliography

Chapman, Gary. Excerpt from The Five Love Languages. http://www.fivelovelanguages.com/learn.html (viewed 7/13/08)

Sandford, John Loren, and Paula Sandford. The Transformation of the Inner Man. Pretoria: Van Schaik Uitgewers, 2000.

Sandford, John Loren, and Paula Sandford. Healing the Wounded Spirit. New York: Victory House, Incorporated, 1985.

Sandford, John Loren, and Mark Sandford. A Comprehensive Guide to Deliverance and Inner Healing. Grand Rapids: Revell, 1992.

Valentino, Jack. Sword of the Spirit School of Prayer & Deliverance Guide. Powder Springs: Sword of the Spirit Healing Ministries, Inc. Unpublished.

Walters, Kathie. Elitism and the False Shepherding Spirit. Macon: Good News Fellowship Ministires, 2001.

Wright, Henry W. A More Excellent Way Be In Health Pathways of Wholeness Spiritual Roots of Disease. Thomaston: Pleasant Valley Publications, 2003.

Unless otherwise noted, all scripture quotations are from:
1) New King James Version of the Bible Copyright ©1979, 1980, 1982 by Thomas Nelson Inc., publishers.
2) The Amplified Bible Copyright © 1965, 1987 by the Zondervan Corporation The Amplified New testament copyright © 1958, 1987 by the Lockman Foundation. Used by permission.

2640536

Made in the USA